ZOW

^MA

THE G SPOT

D0378195

"Many women will want to test this theory themselves. . . .
An intriguing discovery, an intriguing book."
—Barbara Seaman, author of
Free and Female and *The Doctor's
Case Against the Pill*

"By stressing diversity in female sexual response, this book
helps to move us toward an era in which all the meaning-
less shame, confusion, and uncertainty in female sexuality
will melt away, and women can finally accept their feelings and understand why they feel what they feel."
—Josephine Singer, author of
"Types of Female Orgasms" from the
Journal of Sexual Response

"Bound to generate a stir." —*Kirkus Reviews*

"Brimming with research findings and case histories. . . .
Based on their cautiously presented findings, women and
men appear to be more alike sexually than had been previously imagined." —*Publishers Weekly*

"I found it impossible to put down. It presents its findings in a readable, accessible way, without ever losing sight of the human behind sexuality. I think it is a valuable contribution to the literature on sexuality. Not only am I planning to tell everybody I know about it, but I am going to include it in the bibliography for the course I teach to midwifery students."

> —Ronnie Lichtman, certified nurse midwife,
> co-author of the forthcoming
> *Family Health History Workbook*

"The book provides necessary information in a straightforward manner." *—Library Journal*

"A scientific eyewitness case for the vaginal orgasm and female ejaculation . . . they're taking on not only Alfred Kinsey but Masters and Johnson . . . all of whom have maintained that female orgasm is solely a product of clitoral stimulation, and all of whom are viewed as the oracle at Delphi by those who study sex." *—Playboy*

QUANTITY SALES

Most Dell books are available at special quantity discounts when purchased in bulk by corporations, organizations, or groups. Special imprints, messages, and excerpts can be produced to meet your needs. For more information, write to: Dell Publishing, 1540 Broadway, New York, NY 10036. Special Markets.

INDIVIDUAL SALES

Are there any Dell books you want but cannot find in your local stores? If so, you can order them directly from us. You can get any Dell book currently in print. For a complete up-to-date listing of our books and information on how to order, write to: Dell Readers Service, Box DR, 1540 Broadway, New York, NY 10036.

THE G SPOT

And Other Recent Discoveries About Human Sexuality

ALICE KAHN LADAS, M.S.S., Ed.D.

BEVERLY WHIPPLE, R.N., M.Ed.

JOHN D. PERRY, M.Div., Ph.D.

A DELL BOOK

For our silent partner
Harold Ladas

Published by
Dell Publishing
a division of
Bantam Doubleday Dell Publishing Group, Inc.
1540 Broadway
New York, New York 10036

The extract from *Sex: The Facts, the Acts and Your Feelings* by Michael
Carrera is reprinted with kind permission of the author and the publishers in
North America, Crown Publishers, Inc., © Mitchell Beazley Publishers,
1981, text © Michael Carrera, 1981.

The excerpt from *The Inner Game of Tennis* by W. Timothy Gallwey,
Copyright © 1974, is reprinted with kind permission of Random House, Inc.

Material from the *Journal of Sex Research* has been used with kind
permission of the *Journal*, a publication of the Society for the Scientific
Study of Sex.

Illustrations 1, 2, 3, 4, and 6 by Jean G. Addiego
Illustration 5 by Laura Hartman

ISBN: 0-440-13040-9

Reprinted by arrangement with Holt, Rinehart and Winston
Printed in the United States of America
September 1983

20   19   18   17   16

OPM

Evasion of instruction concerning anatomy in action is in part responsible for the physical discords alleged to be the original cause for half the mental maladjustments and three-quarters of the divorces and desertions.... Many of our present beliefs concerning average sex experiences and normal sex life have the status of surmise standing on foundations no more secure than general impressions and scattered personal histories.

ROBERT LATOU DICKINSON, M.D.
1933

Contents

List of Illustrations

Acknowledgments

There is no adequate way to thank the thousands of people who shared their experiences with us through interviews, letters, and questionnaires. They know who they are and may recognize their contributions.

There is certainly no adequate way to thank Bobbi Mark. She is the kind of editor writers dream about with nostalgia for the "good old days." From the start, her commitment to this project has been total and included, in addition, a profound understanding of the field of sexology, sustained editorial creativity, and painstaking time-consuming help with line-by-line editing.

Thanks to our excellent agent, Heide Lange, who helped us find Bobbi and guided us skillfully through the confusing labyrinths of the publishing world.

We thank our "silent" partner, Harold Ladas, for his perspective on the history of science and research, his effectiveness in resolving conflicts, his astuteness as a business manager, and his diligent attention to the details of writing, research, and business.

Without Bobbi, Heide, and Harold, this book would not exist.

We also thank Alberta and George Sellmer, Josephine Singer, and Barbara Scheufele for reading the manuscript and offering valuable suggestions, Jim Whipple for the many hours night and day he put into this project, George Bach for his encouragement and for introducing us to Heide, Pat Stevenson, our excellent and obliging typist, Magda Gottesman of the Hunter College Library, Jean Addiego for her excellent illustrations, and Catherine Donovan for her secretarial help.

We are standing on the shoulders of many pioneers and professionals, some celebrated, some less well known or unknown, and would like to acknowledge our debt to a few of them: Freud, Dickenson, Havelock Ellis, Wilhelm Reich, Ernst Gräfenberg, Kinsey et al., Arnold Kegel, Masters and Johnson, Alexander Lowen, Edward Brecher, Josephine and Irving Singer, J. Lowndes Sevely, J. W. Bennett, Edwin Belzer, Jr., Frank Addiego, and Helen Robinson.

For their constant and loving support throughout the entire project and their patience with a preoccupied wife and mother, Alice Ladas thanks her husband, Harold, and their daughters, Robin and Pamela.

Beverly Whipple would like to express her sincere thanks to her husband, Jim, and their children, Allen and Susan, for their personal support, encouragement, and love, and to her dear friends and colleagues Frank Addiego and Michael Perry for their professional support, encouragement, and suggestions.

John Perry wishes to acknowledge the many and varied contributions of Carolyn G. Perry, who supported research and development of vaginal myography from the very beginning, Madeline Daniels, who provided opportunities to expand clinical knowledge at Crossroads Center in New Hampshire, and the Biofeedback Society of New England, which invited and heard the first professional paper on vaginal myography in 1978.

Introduction

This book is about important newly discovered facts that are crucial to our understanding of how human beings function sexually. We believe that the information presented here can be used to help millions of women and men lead more pleasurable and satisfying lives and avoid a good deal of unnecessary suffering and frustration.

Some of these facts were already known but were ignored or rejected because they did not fit into what was culturally or scientifically acceptable and were not connected with each other in a meaningful way. "Facts are of no value," said Charles Darwin, "unless they are for or against some point of view." Considered in relation to each other, the facts presented profoundly alter our understanding of human sexuality.

This is not a book about love. It is not about the problems people have in relating to one another. It is not about resolving emotional problems, although some of them may vanish as the facts described are applied to people's lives. Above all, this book is not a panacea for all of the sexual problems faced by humankind. On the other hand, the evidence we present indicates that women and men are more alike sexually than had been previously imagined. This may help to remove barriers between people and bring about a greater understanding of human sexual behavior.

These findings constitute an important step in demystifying Freud's "dark continent," which is not quite as dark as it was when he coined that phrase in connection with female sexuality one hundred years ago. But much more research remains to be done. If these new findings are in accord with your beliefs, habits, and attitudes, you will react to them and apply them differently than if they conflict with what you have been taught or are accustomed to doing.

We do not expect anyone to accept what we are saying unconditionally, nor do we want them to. We hope the information will be considered, validated, or rejected, depending on experience, and acted upon where appropriate. We also hope that it will be subjected to rigorous scientific scrutiny. This book is not intended primarily for the scientific community but for everyone who is interested in human sexuality. For those who wish to further investigate the scientific evidence, additional technical information is provided in the reference notes and appendixes.

Theoretically, information can be considered by itself. In practice, however, it cannot be separated from the personal and social context in which it is received. Therefore, in addition to offering information, we hope that this book will provide support for many of our readers who have been denying their perceptions of their own bodies in an effort to conform to whatever beliefs about sexuality that have been foisted upon them.

For example, a woman brought up to believe that only men ejaculate may conclude that she is ill, weird, or in some other way defective if she does ejaculate. Just reading this book may offer her enough support to affirm her own experience. If someone else reads the book with her, that is even better. Research has shown that it takes only one supportive person to help most individuals stand up against group pressure.[1]

One way the opinions of others affect us, especially if they are disapproving, is that they cause us anxiety, which often produces undesirable physiological reactions in our bodies. Although the particular manifestations vary from person to person, anxiety tends to alter the functioning of the autonomic nervous system, and sexual behavior is intimately connected with autonomic functioning. Sometimes we are exposed, simultaneously, to information which is contradictory. We have been in that position with regard to female sexuality for at least the last thirty years. Contradictory information creates confusion. When it concerns such an intimate aspect of our lives as sexual expression, it is also likely to create a lot of anxiety.

One reason for writing this book is to reduce that dissonance and achieve the integration and understanding that these new findings make possible. By providing this information, we do not wish to establish a sexual Olympics with new and ever more demanding standards of performance. That would also evoke anxiety and is exactly the opposite of what we have in mind. These findings confirm a variety of sexual experience and refute the contradictory either/or orthodoxies which have produced such dissension and distress in recent years. There is not one ideal way but a continuum of experiences. If you want to move along that continuum in one direction or another, we hope that you will be able to use the information in this book to help you enhance your pleasure and reinforce your feelings of self-worth.

THE G SPOT

· 1 ·

A New Synthesis

Three times in this century, great pioneers in the field of human sexuality have shocked, informed, and transformed our world. The people responsible for these seismic changes are Sigmund Freud, Alfred Kinsey and his co-workers, and the team of Masters and Johnson. They influenced us in far more significant ways than many of us may realize. Their work has significantly shaped our attitudes, influenced our behavior, and changed our lives in many ways; however, their findings and their theoretical conclusions contradict each other, which leaves us in a very real dilemma. Freud told us that the mature woman is vaginally responsive and should give up her childish interest in her clitoris. Kinsey and co-workers, and more recently Masters and Johnson, assured us that orgasm in all women involves the clitoris and that it is the main focus of female erotic arousal.

In the twentieth century, when human sexuality became a legitimate subject for scientific study for the very first time in Western history, how did it happen that the major contributors to this new branch of knowledge were in such sharp disagreement with each other? How could "scientific" research lead in such diametrically opposite directions?

Lest these questions seem abstract or without real impact on the lives of everyday people, let's consider the plight of Joan, typical of thousands of women who became young adults in the 1940s and 1950s.

Joan turned twenty-one during the chaos of World War II. She had dated a number of men, but the one who attracted her most deeply was a captain in the Navy who had volunteered for duty on a submarine chaser off the Atlantic Coast. She gave him her virginity one weekend while he was on shore leave. After that, they exchanged passionate love letters and, during his next leave, were married in Annapolis by a Navy chaplain. Joan and her husband had two children, one while he was at sea and one after the war ended, when they were sharing an apartment in Washington with another couple, who had married under similar circumstances. But Joan was miserable. Her captain, so glamorous while he was in the Navy, had turned out to be an adventurer and a gambler, operating just this side of the law. Unprepared to deal with such a life, Joan had sought the help of a psychoanalyst. That undertaking, which lasted six years, produced two major results: Joan filed for divorce, and also became deeply convinced of her own sexual inadequacy, for she had never, in all of her marriage, except for that very first weekend, experienced an orgasm through intercourse. Her husband had taunted her about this. Her analyst made things worse by telling her that it was a mark of arrested development that

*showed itself in other ways as well. Although Joan
had learned to masturbate to orgasm, she felt it was
wrong to ask her husband to pleasure her in this
"immature" fashion, a fear that was heavily reinforced by her husband and her analyst. For the next
thirty years, until she consulted another therapist
because of a mild depression precipitated by the loss
of a lover, she never found the courage to tell sub-
sequent suitors or anyone else what she enjoyed sexually. Convinced that she would betray her imma-
turity and inadequacy, she spent most of her life
denying her sexuality.*

For every woman like Joan, who had personal experience
with a Freudian psychoanalyst, there are many thousands more
who, without being aware of it, have been similarly influenced
by the followers of Sigmund Freud, for the work of that Viennese physician has trickled down to all levels of our culture and
his concepts have become household words. "Maybe she
unconsciously locked that door." "He's got an enormous *ego*."
"*Oedipus* Schmedipus, just as long as he loves his mother." "Be
careful, your *id* is showing." Such remarks are commonplace
and made by people from all walks of life.

In contrast to Joan, consider Melanie, who went for help to
a counseling clinic in Phoenix, Arizona. Melanie became sexually active in the 1960s, twenty years later than Joan, at a time
when the Beatles were celebrating psychedelic drugs in songs
like "Lucy in the Sky with Diamonds," young people were telling us to make love not war, and Masters and Johnson were
writing about their revolutionary direct observation of sexual
activity in the laboratory. Lest you imagine that we had left
Victorianism behind forever, consider also that most everything pertaining to human sexuality was still listed in the psy-

chological and sociological abstracts under the heading of "criminal deviance."[1]

> *Melanie had lived in a commune in the California redwoods and had experimented with nudity and vegetarianism while trying to live off the land. Group sex had also been a part of her experience. Now she had fallen in love and after living with her man for six months was planning to marry him. "But it wouldn't be fair," she informed her counselor, "because something is wrong with me sexually. I don't like him to touch or kiss my genitals. And that's what I'm supposed to enjoy. I don't like oral sex, and I don't even like my lover's penis to touch my clitoris. I like to be penetrated from behind, to make love intensely with a lot of movement. Something is terribly wrong with me. I reach orgasm too quickly and in the wrong way. I am not normal."*

Melanie felt abnormal because she did not like clitoral stimulation. Joan felt uncomfortable because she did. The fears of both women were perpetuated, if not generated, by conflicting popular beliefs of the day. For the past thirty years, many of us have lived with these or similar contradictory and confusing views. To help understand how this strange polarization could come about, let's take a closer look at the controversy that arose between the Freudians and the sex researchers, and at the people who helped to create it.

A hundred years ago, public discussion of sexual pleasure and sexuality was not acceptable. Scientists who tried to study sex were considered suspect by their peers, and they often feared for their reputations. (To a large extent this problem is still with us.) Victorianism, characterized by one writer as a "sexually debilitating disease," was in full swing. While the Victorian age produced some remarkable pornography in which women were portrayed as enjoying sex very much indeed, the official view of the day was better expressed by Lord Acton, who wrote, "Happily for society the idea that women possess sexual feelings can be put aside as a vile aspersion." According to the prevailing view, lack of sexual desire was an important aspect of femininity. The Victorian concept of a woman's function is clearly stated in a handbook for dutiful wives and mothers written in the 1840s:

> The peculiar province of woman is to tend with patient assiduity around the bed of sickness; to watch the feeble steps of infancy; to communicate to the young the elements of knowledge; and bless with smiles those of their friends who are declining in the vale of tears.[2]

Her role as an active sexual partner is underplayed, to put it mildly.

Queen Victoria championed these ideas and actively prevented women from entering into the professions, particularly into medicine. The Victorian expectation was that women should attend to being dutiful wives and mothers. The librettos of Gilbert and Sullivan's operettas are filled with pathetic older women who have no place in society and are economically bereft when not under the care of a male. One of Freud's professional colleagues, German neuropsychiatrist Richard von Krafft-Ebing, a noted writer on the subject of sexual pathology, regarded sexuality itself as a kind of loathsome disease. He had this to say about women:

> If she is normally developed mentally and well-bred, her sexual desire is small. If this were not so, the

whole world would become a brothel and marriage and a family impossible. It is certain that the man that avoids women and the woman that seeks men are abnormal.[3]

Such a milieu hardly seems an encouraging one in which to begin investigating the sexual nature of man, let alone of woman, yet that is one of Freud's major accomplishments.

Freud was born in what is now Czechoslovakia, in 1856, just sixteen years after Queen Victoria married her beloved Albert. Freud's family moved to Vienna when he was four years old and his entire education took place in that great cultural center. In order to support his wife and children, he gave up a career in laboratory research and became a neurologist in private practice. As he explained at the age of eighty:

I discovered some important new facts about the unconscious and the psychic life, the role of instinctual urges, and so on. Out of these findings, grew a new science, psychoanalysis, a part of psychology, as the new method of treatment of the neuroses. I had to pay heavily for this bit of good luck. People did not believe in my facts and thought my theories unsavory. Resistance was strong and unrelenting.[4]

Freud's investigations shocked the Western world and resulted in his exclusion from many of the learned societies which had initially welcomed him as an innovator. His crimes were that he challenged the prevailing concept of man as a rational being and claimed that the libido (sex drive) was responsible for much of human behavior. Comparing the mind to an iceberg, largely submerged and invisible, he told us that the greater part of the mind is irrational and unconscious, with only the tip of the preconscious and conscious showing above the surface. He maintained that the larger, unconscious part—much of it sexual—is more important in guiding our lives than the rational part, even though we deceive ourselves into believing it is the other way around.

He taught therapists a new way of treating patients, to listen to their free associations and dreams as a means of learning more about them and helping them. He called attention to the crucial importance of the first few years of life and the relationship of the child to its early environment. He was the first to tell us about childhood sexuality and to show us how, in that respect as in many others, "The child is father of the Man."

In addition to these enormously important contributions, he taught us many other things about human nature and sexuality. Although not everyone agrees with it, Freud and many others regarded his theory of the repressed Oedipus complex as one of his major achievements. In simplest terms, this theory states that the child's first erotic object is its mother, and for both boys and girls the mother becomes the prototype of all later love objects.

As the little boy begins to experience pleasure in his genitals, he desires to become his mother's seducer and to replace his father. Because his father is bigger and stronger, he knows that he will fail. Besides, he needs his father. At the same time, his mother tries to stop the little boy from masturbating. If she fails, she may go so far as to threaten that something terrible will happen if he persists in this bad habit. Should the little boy happen to see a woman's genitals and fantasize that her penis has been removed as a punishment, he may develop a fear of castration. This, according to Freud, may lead to a host of other "neurotic symptoms," such as a fear of self-assertion (in order to avoid this dreaded punishment) or its counterpart, defiance of authority (i.e. the father—since the best defense may be attack). It may also cause excessive dependence on the mother because of fear of the father, revulsion for the "castrated" woman, or a combination of the two. This, in turn, can sometimes lead to later avoidance of women through celibacy or homosexuality. These attitudes lie dormant in the boy's unconscious, ready to be reactivated by events in later life and to interfere with his sexuality as it emerges in puberty and develops in adulthood.

The girl, according to Freud, evolves differently. Since she doesn't have a penis to begin with, she doesn't fear losing it. Instead she envies boys and rather than having castration anxieties, she develops penis envy. She can try to emulate boys, and if that attitude persists, she may become a homosexual. Or she may try to compensate for her lack, developing instead what Freud regarded as a "normal feminine attitude"—passive, compliant, and dependent. Another problem the girl may face is that of remaining angry with her mother for having given her such a deficient girl's body. This attitude, according to Freud, is the origin of the Electra complex, and the girl tries to take the mother's place with her father. All of these feelings are, of course, repressed, since people who harbor them strenuously resist their return to consciousness. According to the Freudians, this accounts for the fact that his ideas seem outlandish or repellent and are rejected by many people. It becomes a complicated and challenging task to differentiate between what is rejected because it is unconscious and what is rejected because it is untrue.

Based on the presumed inferiority of women and the assumption that the basic prototype for human beings is masculine, Freud went on to develop theories about women's sexuality that gave rise to the sort of cultural attitudes that strongly affected Joan so many years later. He saw the clitoris as a protruding "masculine" organ, a vestigial, inferior penis. Being more accessible than the vagina, it is naturally discovered first by little girls in their play and self-exploration. Freud theorized that as a girl matures and becomes a woman, she must give up her childish interest in her clitoris and "transfer" the focus of her pleasurable feelings to her vagina. (The vagina is a receptive organ and women are supposed to be receptive.) This came to be known as the "clitoral-vaginal transfer theory."

Many of Freud's theories are accepted today as valid. In fact, he is regarded as one of the creative giants of all time, with good reason. It is easy to criticize great men while standing on their shoulders to view the future. That is not our intention. But the fact is that Freud, in spite of his great contributions, made some significant errors. Those errors are related to the limitations of his research methods and of his own awareness, and the simple fact that a number of findings in social psychology and anthropology that were to influence Freud's followers were still in the future.

Many of his disciples forgot that Freud himself was aware of the limitations of his understanding about female sexuality. Expressing the hope that women analysts might one day shed more light on the subject, he said, "If you want to know more about femininity you must interrogate your own experience, or turn to the poets, or else wait until science can give you more profound and more coherent information."[5]

Like the rest of us, Freud was influenced by his own unconscious, partly related to the peculiar circumstances of his personal and family history, and partly because of the patriarchal cultural climate in which he was raised. At that time, it was more permissible to talk about males as sexual beings than it was to discuss women's sexual pleasure.

Freud's method of scientific inquiry was in part responsible both for his revolutionary theories and his errors. He wrote that the principles of psychoanalysis were based both on his personal and clinical experiences—that is, on his introspective examination of his own thoughts and feelings as well as his observations of his patients and interpretations of them. His view was that no one who had not made similar observations was in a position to judge his ideas. That view still persists today among many neo-Freudians.

Freud based his theories on a relatively small group of private patients he studied extensively and who were, because of their interest in trying this new form of therapy and their ability to pay for it, not necessarily representative of people in the Viennese society of that day, let alone of all human beings. Anthropologist Margaret Mead, by contrast, studied the sexual habits of ordinary people in dozens of societies and taught us the valuable lesson that other cultures have different ways of doing things. She taught us that it would be provincial for us to assume that "our" way is the only "right" one.

Freud and his followers were basically uncritical of society, and they accepted the Victorian idea of male supremacy. Nevertheless, from the start, their movement attracted many extremely able and productive women. A few made important contributions, but only one of the early group dared to challenge the patriarch. The rest managed to fit their sexual experiences and those of their female patients into the mold cast for them by Freud.

The exception was Karen Horney, M.D., who began to challenge Freud's assumptions as early as 1924. Though he was willing to concede that his own understanding of female sexuality might be limited, Freud did not take kindly to disagreement. He tolerated Horney's digressions until 1938 when he announced that "a woman analyst who has not been sufficiently convinced of her own desire for a penis also fails to assign adequate importance to that factor in her patients!"[6]

What aroused him to make such a statement? Horney had begun to think about feminine psychology in the mid-1920s and she took issue with Freud on a number of points. Unlike Freud, she also acknowledged the influence of culture, which at that time forced women to adapt themselves to the wishes of men and to view this adaptation as a reflection of their true nature. She spoke about women's capacity for motherhood as evidence of their physiological superiority, and she spoke about men's envy of that function. She also considered evidence that the vagina as well as the clitoris plays a part in the infantile genital organization of women. In a paper written in 1926, she had concluded by saying:

> . . . my primary intention . . . was to indicate a possible source of error arising out of the sex of the observer, and by doing so to make a step forward . . . to get beyond the subjectivity of the masculine or the feminine standpoint. . . . [7]

When Horney arrived in the United States, as a non-Jewish refugee from Hitler, her proclivity for seeing things in their cultural context was greatly reinforced by the work of cultural anthropologists Ruth Benedict and Margaret Mead and the psychiatrist Harry Stack Sullivan. Horney began to view neurosis as an interaction of biological and societal factors. Her views about the importance of culture as well as her disbelief in anatomy as destiny were fully supported by Mead's pioneering work. Horney was familiar with American psychology, which emphasized the role of learning and helped her explain the cultural differences she had observed. Mead concluded that the capacity for orgasm is a learned response, which a given culture may or may not help its women to develop. For example, the Mundugumor, a tribal people of New Guinea, believe in orgasm for the woman while the neighboring Arapesh do not. Mundugumor women are typically orgasmic and Arapesh women are mostly anorgasmic. The capacity for orgasm involves a number of culturally learned responses. For a woman to develop this innate capacity, she needs to know about the physical aspects of her sexual response and must also receive appropriate stimulation. Only in those societies that teach their members effective techniques do women learn to achieve sexual climax. (This certainly is a persuasive argument for the publication of the "new" information in this book about areas especially responsive to sexual stimulation.)

It was not until the 1950s, when biologist Alfred Kinsey, Ph.D., began to study the sexual habits of men and women in our own culture using quantitative methods, that we became aware of the enormous variability in sexual behavior, even within our own culture. One result of Kinsey's work was that Freud's clitoral-vaginal transfer theory began to be officially challenged. There were, of course, millions of women all along who had experienced clitoral pleasure, but they hadn't said much about it publicly.

No science can move forward without the application of quantitative measurement. In order to be unbiased about our observations, it is essential to count and measure large numbers of people. This is true even of so intimate a science as sexology. Not only did Kinsey introduce quantitative methods, he also effectively employed statistics in the service of human sexuality with the same precision and astuteness that he had used in his previous scientific endeavors. Freud did not really understand how to use statistics effectively or how to design an experiment with human subjects, and some of his more serious errors arose from the failure to test his theories using these methods.

For example, there was a time in his career when Freud believed that having intercourse while using a condom was one direct cause of what he called "actual neurosis." But he never studied couples who had similar problems and did not use condoms. As one sex historian, Edward Brecher, observed, "Statistics may err on occasion: but those who eschew statistics inevitably err very often."[8]

Kinsey largely relied on structured interviews and developed that art to a highly sophisticated degree. He also taught a devoted staff how to interview, how to tailor the questions to the backgrounds of the subjects, and what to look for. As one of his interviewees later wrote, "My wife and I . . . came away with the same impression of superb craftmanship. Comparing notes afterward, we agreed that [Kinsey's associate] Dr. Pomeroy's transparent honesty towards us had developed in us an almost compulsive need to be completely honest with him. Any omissions from the answers we supplied were attributable solely to the limitations of our memories."[9] It was a gigantic task, and Kinsey himself carried the largest part of the burden. He had collected more than 7,000 of the approximately 17,000 case histories that were completed at the time of his death.

We learned a lot about human sexual behavior from those interviews, which were far more comprehensive than any previously undertaken. In a lecture at the New York Academy of Medicine in 1955, shortly before Kinsey's death, a packed house filled with prestigious members of the medical profession heard Kinsey talk about the wide variety of male and female sexual behavior. Heated debates ensued about the reliability of Kinsey's data, which in effect pulled the rug out from under the Victorians by revealing that more people were enjoying more different forms of sex, including masturbation, homosexuality, anal intercourse, and especially extramarital sex, than society was willing to acknowledge publicly. So they tried to attack his accuracy and representativeness.

But as time went by it was generally accepted that, while not valid in every respect, his data were the most reliable in existence and tended to understate rather than overstate the facts. They certainly brought into the open a whole range of human behavior that had previously been discussed only in whispers behind closed doors, if at all.

Like Freud, and all other great pioneers, Kinsey made some errors. One, which directly affects our current dilemma, grew out of his desire to be as scientifically objective as possible. In a special research project initiated by the Kinsey Institute an attempt was made to find out which areas of a woman's genitals are most sensitive to sexual stimulation. Three male and two female gynecologists tested more than 800 women by touching sixteen points, including the clitoris, labia (major and minor), vaginal lining, and cervix.[10] They didn't want to touch the subjects directly because they were afraid of being less than impersonal and scientific, so they used a device similar to a Q-tip.[11] Unfortunately, sensitive areas of the vagina, we now know, respond to deep pressure but not to soft touch, and so the Kinsey researchers concluded, erroneously, that the clitoris is sensitive and the vagina is not.

Encouraged by the scientific progress made through Kinsey's pioneering work, Masters and Johnson took the final courageous step and decided to observe sex firsthand in the laboratory and then report their findings.

Not only does science require that observations be measured and quantified, but it also requires firsthand observation. For example, Aristotle believed that a weight ten times as heavy as another would drop ten times as fast. According to a legend, many centuries later Galileo tested Aristotle's belief by dropping two such weights from the leaning tower of Pisa, demonstrating that two unequal weights actually hit the ground simultaneously.

It wasn't until Masters and Johnson reported their direct observations of masturbation and intercourse that we were able to understand with any clarity what happens to the human body as a result of erotic stimulation. For ease of understanding, they divided the sexual response cycle into four phases: excitement, plateau, orgasm, and resolution.

In the excitement phase, a woman's first physiological response is vaginal lubrication and a man's is penile erection. Lubrication is like erection in that it occurs as a result of the increase in blood supply, which in turn causes engorgement of surrounding tissues. Among the other changes in this phase are the swelling or erection of the nipples in many women and some men.

In the plateau phase (actually an advanced stage of excitement), the tissues in the outer third of the vagina swell and reduce the diameter of the opening, allowing it to grip the penis, while in men the testes grow larger and are pulled up toward the pelvic floor. The clitoris also retracts and draws away from the vaginal entrance, becoming more difficult to find. Muscular tension increases in both women and men.

In the phase which Masters and Johnson call orgasmic, there is in women a series of rhythmic contractions of the "orgasmic platform," the outer third of the vagina and the tissues and muscles surrounding it. These are muscular contractions which at first occur at intervals of about four-fifths of a second. Then the interval lengthens and the intensity of the contractions decreases. According to Masters and Johnson, an intense orgasm has eight to twelve contractions while a milder one has only three to five. Objectively the experience of orgasm begins when the first muscle spasm occurs. The uterus also contracts rhythmically. The reaction of men is similar, except that there is, in addition, a complex process usually leading to ejaculation that Masters and Johnson described in detail, but only for men. In both women and men, there are changes that occur in the rest of the body during orgasm. The pulse increases, blood pressure elevates, and the breathing rate accelerates. Muscles throughout the body may contract and then relax. Sometimes there is a skin flush or blushing over much of the body.

In the fourth and final stage, resolution, the organs gradually return to their unstimulated condition. The resolution phase is shortest after a single orgasm, takes a bit longer after multiple orgasm, and lasts longer still when there has been no orgasm following the excitement and plateau stages.

Again there was a problem in research methodology, an error that resulted from the shortcomings of Kinsey's studies and led directly to the dilemma we are considering. Partly because of Kinsey's work, Masters and Johnson assumed that the ability to masturbate to orgasm by stimulating the clitoris was the hallmark of normal female sexual response. Therefore, the ability to masturbate to orgasm in this manner became one of their criteria for the selection of research subjects. We now realize that they overlooked women who function differently.

This may have been why Masters and Johnson took the position that they did in the long-standing debate about clitoral versus vaginal orgasm. All female orgasms, according to them, involve the clitoris and are physiologically indistinguishable. They believed that any perceived difference is a subjective one because all orgasms in the female involve contact with other parts of the female introitus (opening of the vagina). This generates friction between the clitoris and its own hood. The same friction that occurs during masturbation may also occur during intercourse.

Remember that Freud believed there are two kinds of orgasm, one resulting from clitoral stimulation, which he regarded as masculine and immature, and the other resulting from vaginal penetration, which he regarded as mature and feminine. Some adherents to the Freudian viewpoint carried his views to an extreme, labeling any woman who only responded clitorally as frigid and neurotic. A renowned obstetrician actually advised a large group of men to use only penile penetration with their wives, so as not to get them "stuck" on their clitoris. At the opposite end of the spectrum, Masters and Johnson's findings released a flood of literature extolling the virtues of the clitoris. Various factions within the women's movement took up the cry in some of their writings, questioning why any heterosexual woman would bother with intercourse at all, except for purposes of procreation. Any woman (or man) who had personally experienced only one way of functioning—whichever one—could take their experiences and their subjective views to logical but contradictory extremes. But what about women who continued to experience both?

In light of Freud's dictum that clinical observations only become meaningful when viewed against the background of personal experience, it may be helpful to consider a recent survey of women bioenergetic analysts. Bioenergetic Analysis, founded by Alexander Lowen, M.D., is a neo-Freudian body-oriented therapy that grew out of the clinical work of Freud's pupil Wilhelm Reich. Unlike most psychotherapies, Bioenergetic Analysis works directly with breathing and muscle tension, as well as with words. People involved in this type of therapy may lie down (a passive position conducive to free association and fantasy), sit (a position that facilitates relating to others), or stand (a more adult, assertive, and stressful position). Although sexologists often use the terms *climax* and *orgasm* interchangeably, bioenergetic analysts use the term *cli-*

max to describe muscular contractions localized in the genitals and the word *orgasm* to describe contractions that spread throughout the entire body.

In 1975, at a conference organized by the Institute for Bioenergetic Analysis, women met separately from their male colleagues for the first time. It occurred to some that in all their years of personal and supervisory therapy with men they had never dealt clearly with their feelings about being women. Although many questions were raised at their meetings, few conclusions were reached, and the women failed to express what was on their minds and in their hearts. This is not difficult to understand, even in the late 1970s, since they were all members of a professional group run by men with plenty of unspoken rules about what they ought to be and do.

If the women could not express their views publicly to one another, perhaps they could do so privately in writing. Thus Alice and Harold Ladas decided to send out an anonymous questionnaire. A second reason for the questionnaire was to see whether it would bring to the surface differences between bioenergetic theory (circa 1977) and the actual beliefs, practices, and experiences of the women involved with it, something similar to what Karen Horney had been trying to do in the 1920s. Since all of the writing and lecturing on Bioenergetic Analysis had been done by men, based on clinical observation and philosophical speculation, it seemed time to get objective confirmation and some feedback from the women themselves.

The protective anonymity of the questionnaire gave the women bioenergetic analysts a chance to reveal many important things about their personal and professional experiences, and to discuss their theoretical agreements and differences freely. Close to seventy percent of the 198 women responded. The most significant theoretical disagreements involved the importance of the clitoris, a word not mentioned in their meetings, possibly because they had been taught that if they were to be considered mature, they wouldn't want to admit that the clitoris still held interest for them.

According to Freud, only persons who had experienced the analytic method personally and had made analytic observations of others would be in a position to evaluate his theories adequately. The women bioenergetic analysts were the first group in history who met Freud's criteria to be asked for their views. Additionally they fulfilled another of Freud's criteria—that their analyses be successful. Over eighty percent of the female therapists in this study reported that they had been helped by therapy in a number of important ways. Admission to a formal training program adds credence to the success of their analyses and their subjective evaluation of themselves. Eighty-one percent reported reaching orgasm through intercourse. Nevertheless, eighty-seven percent disagreed with the statement, "Stimulation of the clitoris directly or indirectly in intercourse is not important for the mature woman."[12]

A major conclusion of this survey then is to challenge Freud's clitoral-vaginal transfer theory. According to the respondents, women would prefer not to abandon the clitoris in favor of the vagina, but instead to add vaginal responsiveness to their enjoyment of clitoral stimulation!

Another important difference concerned the women's reports about multiple climax. According to Lowen, multiple climaxes are not true orgasmic experiences, but superficial genital reactions. Yet a majority of these women classified their "multiple climaxes" as "orgasmic" in nature—in spite of the official doctrine.

How can we explain these seemingly contradictory statements? Here is a group of women therapists, many who have experienced personally what it means to have a "vaginal" orgasm—an experience centered in the vagina—yet this same group insists that the clitoris is also significant, that clitoral stimulation during intercourse is pleasurable, that the clitoral orgasm provides a satisfying release and that their partners should help them achieve this when it is desired.

The opinions of the women therapists in this study supported the beliefs of the Freudians and neo-Freudians about the existence of vaginal orgasm as well as the views of the sex researchers about the desirability of clitoral stimulation. Masters and Johnson's notion, however, that *all* orgasms involve the clitoris was not confirmed by the subjective experience of most of the respondents. So again we see that either/or arguments often meet our need for simple answers but rarely succeed in capturing the nature of reality.

Three years later, in 1980, the results of the Ladases' survey were presented by Alice Ladas at the 1980 national meeting of the Society for the Scientific Study of Sex (SSSS). Although the title of their paper was "Freud Through Hite All Partly Right," she also showed how they were also partly wrong. At that same meeting, she first learned about the work of John Perry and Beverly Whipple. New vistas began to open up as common principles emerged.

Alternating at the lectern, each speaking for no longer than five minutes at a time, Perry and Whipple told the conference that:

• There is a spot inside the vagina that is extremely sensitive to deep pressure. It lies in the anterior wall of the vagina about two inches from the entrance. They named this area the Gräfenberg spot, after Dr. Ernst Gräfenberg, the first modern physician to describe it.

• The spot has been found in every woman they had examined.

• When properly stimulated, the Gräfenberg spot swells and leads to orgasm in many women.

• At the moment of orgasm, many women ejaculate a liquid through the urethra that is chemically similar to male ejaculate but contains no sperm.

• As a result of stimulation of the G spot, women often have a series of orgasms.

• For many women it is difficult to properly stimulate the G spot in the missionary position. Other positions work better.

• Using a diaphragm for birth control interferes with stimulation of the G spot in some women.

• Because they believe they are urinating, many women are embarrassed about ejaculating. Thinking the same thing, their partners often belittle them, which is one reason many women have learned to suppress orgasm.

• The strength of a woman's pubococcygeus muscle is directly related to her ability to reach orgasm through intercourse.

• Women can learn to strengthen their pubococcygeus muscles or to relax them if they are too tense.

• If men increase the strength of their pubococcygeus muscles, they too can learn to become multiply orgasmic and separate orgasm from ejaculation.

• There are several types of orgasm in women and men. In women there is a vulval orgasm, triggered by the clitoris, a uterine orgasm, triggered by intercourse, and a combination of the two. In men there is an orgasm triggered by the penis and one by the prostate.

Included in the professional audience at this presentation were Kinsey's colleague, Wardell Pomeroy, Ph.D., Mary Calderone, M.D., executive director of the Sex Information and

Education Council of the United States (SIECUS), and many other well known pioneers in the field of human sexuality.

Although this was not the first time that Perry and Whipple had presented their data, it was a historic moment in the field of sex research and represented a pleasant contrast with the atmosphere of tension and discord that had prevailed during earlier meetings of the society. In 1957, SSSS had sponsored a debate between Albert Ellis, Ph.D., founder of Rational Emotive Therapy, and Alexander Lowen, M.D. Ellis talked about the "myth of the vaginal orgasm," while Lowen asserted that the clitoral orgasm represents one form of orgasmic impotence in the female. This polarization of views was entirely missing from the 1980 meeting. Absent too were the fears that had accompanied the screening in 1958 of a sexually explicit film about the early findings of Masters and Johnson. Among the first films of this nature, it was most impressive, and seemed to demonstrate convincingly that all orgasms involve the clitoris and are physiologically the same. During the screening, there was constant checking to see that no outsiders had slipped in to spy or satisfy pornographic appetites. Yet no one worried about the film that Perry and Whipple showed to support their data.

Upon first learning about the findings of Perry and Whipple, Martin Weisberg, M.D., a gynecologist at Thomas Jefferson University Hospital in Philadelphia, responded, "Bull ... I spend half of my waking hours examining, cutting apart, putting together, removing, or rearranging female reproductive organs. There is no female prostate, and women don't ejaculate."

Yet several hours later, after seeing their film and examining one of the research subjects, he was humming a different tune:

The vulva and vagina were normal with no abnormal masses or spots. The urethra was normal. Everything was normal. She then had her partner stimulate her by inserting two fingers into the vagina and stroking along the urethra lengthwise. To our amazement, the area began to swell. It eventually became a firm one by two cm oval area distinctly different from the rest of the vagina. In a few moments the subject seemed to perform a Valsalva maneuver [bearing down as if starting to defecate] and seconds later several cc's of milky fluid shot out of the urethra. The material was clearly not urine. In fact, if the chemical analysis described in the paper is correct, its composition was closest to prostatic fluid . . .

I was really confused. I checked with several anatomists, all of whom thought I was crazy. But my patients didn't think I was crazy. A few told me that they ejaculate. Some know about the erotic area around the urethra. And *everyone* who went home to experiment found the Gräfenberg spot.

I still have no explanation for this, but I can attest to the fact that the Gräfenberg spot and female ejaculation exist.

Years from now I am sure that a medical school lecturer will joke about how it wasn't until 1980 that the medical community finally accepted the fact that women really do ejaculate.[13]

But in 1982 the greater part of the medical community still does not know about these concepts, and it may be years before the majority of general practitioners or even the majority of obstetricians and gynecologists accept them.

To find out what her professional associates knew about these matters, Alice Ladas designed a second questionnaire in 1981 that was sent to women bioenergetic analysts and circulated at several professional meetings of men and women. It soon became apparent that her colleagues were voting by preference, as if for a candidate at an election, rather than on a matter of scientific fact. At a staff meeting of pastoral counselors, the tally was as follows: four for female ejaculation, four against female ejaculation, three didn't know. Regarding the location of a specially sensitive spot in the vagina, five said that there was one, four said that the vagina itself is not sensitive, and two did not know. Of the five who voted for a sensitive spot, two located it at the entrance to the vagina, one placed it on the cervix, one placed it at the back of the vagina, and one on the anterior wall. This diversity of opinion came from men and women who regularly work with individuals and couples and who consider sexual counseling part of their job. At a meeting of marriage and family counselors, mostly female, the vote was similarly split.

Many of our friends and patients were fascinated by the new information, and a number were personally familiar with these phenomena already. The administrator of a large nonprofit medical organization, a woman of forty-five, told us:

> I've known for a long time that women ejaculate, because of my personal experience. I was embarrassed by it, but I always knew it was natural, and that the fluid was not urine. Compared to the other type of orgasm, one that involves ejaculation is more of a total letting-go. But even though the experience is deeper than the usual type of orgasm, it is much easier to become aroused again.

A twenty-one-year-old said of her first and only lover:

> "Yes, there is a special spot inside. It's in the front and a little to the right of center. When he touches

it with his penis, it's a very pleasurable spot and
much easier to reach when I am on top of him."

A publisher of pornography told us about an employee of
his, a homosexual man, who had written a book that dealt with
female ejaculation. "In my office, they thought it was a joke
and that only a gay man could write such a book. We never
published it."

Said the wife of a Presbyterian minister:

I discovered that special spot first through a man
using his fingers. I thought I had an inverted clitoris
. . . a clitoris inside my vagina. That spot is much
more pleasurable for me than my clitoris, but I'd
heard that the clitoris is the only sensitive place, so
I was puzzled.

A woman whose sexual life started at sixteen reported:

When I was very young, it was frightening. I didn't
know what was happening. When I came it was like
I had peed. We were both just drenched, but I knew
I hadn't peed. It happened only during intercourse
and not when I masturbated. Soon after, though, I
learned about birth control—thank God! And with
a diaphragm, it didn't happen anymore.

A thirty-five-year-old dancer said:

Orgasm hasn't been easy for me. But I have a new
boyfriend, and I care about him a great deal. He
gets much pleasure from anal sex, and I wanted to
please him, so I went along with it. I thought I was

*crazy to do it, and the first time it was painful. But
then, some barrier broke down. I stopped trying to
resist him. It was almost like my bladder was being
touched. There was a feeling like I had to urinate. I
would start to make sounds and to give in to the
sensation. It was a feeling like collapsing inside. The
first time it happened intensely, I got frightened
and ran into the bathroom and started to cry. It felt
like he'd taken something of mine that is private . . .
like he'd gotten into my psyche as well as my body.
It was like a death, and I was confused. That first
time, I didn't feel love, only great intensity, but
since then the tenderness and intensity come
together.*

From a former prostitute, who now works for a nonprofit
educational institution:

*Of course I know women ejaculate. Just ask any les-
bian if you want to know. There are clitoral and
vaginal orgasms, and they are very different. Vaginal orgasms are related to a special very sweet spot
inside the vagina.*

Many men we talked to had experienced the same thing, the
special spot inside of some women, only they weren't quite sure
what it was:

*Each woman has her own individual responses. It's
very hard for a man to really understand exactly
what is happening in a woman. She can be full of
responses, and still a man can be in the dark about
how deep these are. But certain women want you to*

really pound them beyond the cervix in order to come. Don't you think that this pounding and thrusting that some women crave is an attempt to stimulate that spot?

When asked about ejaculation, the same man replied:

Yes, I've heard of it. I was with a girl once, and she came for the very first time in her life, and she ejaculated. She was terribly embarrassed because she thought she had peed. I didn't know any better either. It happened that I knew her quite well and so we saw each other again. If we hadn't been good friends, I might have fled in confusion.

Another man said, "It didn't smell like semen or like pee, and it certainly was a lovely experience. I like to think my wife and I are fairly knowledgeable. So how could we have overlooked this for so long?"

How is it that the medical and psychological professions have overlooked these experiences, which seem to be so familiar but so little discussed? Why is it that anatomists have missed the Gräfenberg spot? Those are hard questions to answer. Clinicians have been free to ask, "Does this hurt, does that hurt?" but they have been reluctant to inquire about the corollary, "Does this feel good, does that feel better?" Dissection of dead tissue may not readily reveal the Gräfenberg spot unless the dissector is specifically searching for it.

Yet there have been many historical references to female ejaculation, beginning with Aristotle, who observed that women expel a fluid during orgasm. And in 1950, Gräfenberg " . . . noted that some women expelled large quantities of clear fluid from the urethra during orgasm." He believed that this fluid was secreted from the intra-urethral glands. In 1978, J. Lowndes Sevely and J. W. Bennett, Ph.D., concluded that some women ejaculate and that the source of that ejaculate is the "female prostate, a system of glands and ducts which surrounds the female urethra and develops from the same embryologic tissue as the male prostate."[14]

Unlike many others, Perry and Whipple did not overlook these reports, but instead began to do their own research to validate them. Their findings are potentially of great value to us all—depending on *how we use them*. As Edwin Belzer, Ph.D., wrote in the *Journal of Sex Research:*

> If objective evidence demonstrating the existence of female ejaculation is found, it could be used in diametrically opposite ways. It could free those who, in deference to the voice of authority, have denied the reality or acceptability of their own experience. Or it could trap those who believe that a woman's orgasm is "imperfect" unless accompanied by ejaculation. Such a belief could cause people either to try to ejaculate or to try to cause ejaculation, considering failure to do so as an indication of sexual inadequacy.[15]

People at the SSSS meeting seemed very excited about Perry and Whipple's report. The Ladases were particularly enthusiastic, especially about the Gräfenberg spot and the different types of female orgasm. These findings could explain the responses of the women bioenergetic therapists who experienced orgasm through intercourse but felt that the clitoris was extremely important as well. It also explained their subjects' views on multiple orgasm.

Perry and Whipple were enthusiastic about the Ladases' work as well. Shortly after the conference, Beverly wrote to

Alice, "We are on the same path, and it seems to be leading to the same place, especially, [the idea of] female orgasm being on a continuum . . ." Thus our collaboration began.

The chapters that follow describe, in detail, the four basic ideas that Perry and Whipple brought to the attention of the sex researchers. They are, in fact, not new theories, but information that has been published and then ignored, as have so many important scientific discoveries in other fields. These four discoveries, the Gräfenberg spot, female ejaculation, the importance of pelvic muscle tone, and the continuum of orgasmic response, unify the findings of the Freudians and other sex researchers into an understandable and consistent whole. Our dilemma is resolved. We now have a new synthesis that validates the experience of both vaginal and clitoral orgasm.

·2·

The Gräfenberg Spot

Of the four discoveries mentioned briefly in chapter one, the Gräfenberg spot ranks first in importance. Although it is less dramatic than female ejaculation, and not as important medically as good muscle tone, the G spot is what specifically frees us from the either/or thinking of the past decades, for it demonstrates that there is not one genital focus of erotic arousal in women, as Masters and Johnson (with help from so many others) have led us to believe. There are, instead, at least two foci—the clitoris and the G spot—just as there are at least two foci in men, the penis and the prostate gland. The clitoris, located outside the body at the entrance to the vagina, is easy for every woman to discover and enjoy by herself. The G spot, located inside the anterior (front) wall of the vagina, is more difficult for a woman to find on her own. The cooperation of a partner is extremely useful, if not essential. The same is true for men. The penis is easy for a man to discover and enjoy by himself, while the prostate, felt through the anterior wall of the rectum, is difficult to locate without the help of a partner.

These facts are well illustrated by the experiences of a couple in their late forties who came for marriage counseling:

The Hoyts had been married for almost twenty years, had two teenaged sons and an eight-year-old daughter. They had been childhood sweethearts, and since their marriage had had a monogamous relationship. The reason they had come for counseling was not that they had any serious problem but because they felt that they were missing something. Sex was good but not as fulfilling an experience as they had hoped. During the first interview, it was clear that there were no serious underlying interpersonal problems, but that the Hoyts had limited the parameters of their sexual behavior. During the second session, they were encouraged to experiment by using their voices during sex and allowing more of their bodies to become involved by deepening their breathing. They were also given information about the location of the G spot and the pleasure that might be elicited through stimulation of Mr. Hoyt's prostate.

This is what he reported on their third visit:

"When I returned home from work, I knew that Ginny had something special in mind. The table was set for two, and the candles were lit. Rebecca was away on a sleep-over, and the two boys were on a camping trip. So I took Ginny into the bedroom, undressed her, and began to massage her all over, carefully avoiding the area around her clitoris on which I had focused for all these years. Instead I began to gently probe her vagina with my fingers . . . something I had not done since our days of petting in the back seat of a car. Turning her on her

tummy, with her feet hanging over the edge of the bed, I immediately located that little oval spot that had been described to us and began to stimulate it firmly with my fingers. Ginny responded with a low moan and then urged me to keep on. "Don't stop," she whispered, and in a very short time, she was gasping with pleasure, and her vagina was pumping my fingers and almost shoving them out. It was wonderfully exciting."

Ginny continued:

"It was overwhelming, and for a short time I could only just rest on the bed, holding Jim and kissing him and saying "Thank you." But soon I recovered, and began to play with his erect penis. Instead of following the pattern which had become almost routine for us, of kissing him and then inserting his penis into my vagina, I ventured into a new place with my tongue and began to kiss Jim between his balls and his anus. It made him gasp, and I knew I had found a new way of pleasing him. Encouraged, I began very gently to insert my finger into his anus, using my own juices for lubrication. Sounds of pleasure from Jim let me know I could continue with this new adventure. I began to stroke Jim's prostate with my finger while kissing him, and had intended to change positions and sit on him before he came, but there wasn't time."

Thus, they both experimented with the pleasure of stimulating new sexual focal points. The Hoyts came in for only one more session after that. Information and a bit of professional support was all they needed to find the excitement and variety that they felt had been missing.

Where exactly is the G spot located? The Gräfenberg Spot lies directly behind the pubic bone within the front wall of the vagina. It is usually located about halfway between the back of the pubic bone and the front of the cervix, along the course of the urethra (the tube through which you urinate) and near the neck of the bladder, where it connects with the urethra. The size and exact location vary. (Imagine a small clock inside the vagina with 12 o'clock pointing towards the navel. The majority of women will find the G spot located in the area between 11 and 1 o'clock.) Unlike the clitoris, which protrudes from the surrounding tissue, it lies deep within the vaginal wall, and a firm pressure is often needed to contact the G spot in its unstimulated state.

As early as 1944, German obstetrician and gynecologist Ernst Gräfenberg collaborated with the prominent American obstetrician and gynecologist Robert L. Dickinson, M.D., who many regard as the first American sexologist. They described a "zone of erogenous feeling" that was "located along the sub-urethral surface of the anterior vaginal wall."[1]

We first read about the existence of this sensitive area in the anterior wall of the vagina from an article written by Gräfenberg in 1950, in which he said:

> . . . an erotic zone could always be demonstrated on the anterior wall of the vagina along the course of the urethra, . . . [which] seems to be surrounded by erectile tissue like the corpora cavernosa [of the penis]. . . . In the course of sexual stimulation, the female urethra begins to enlarge and can be easily

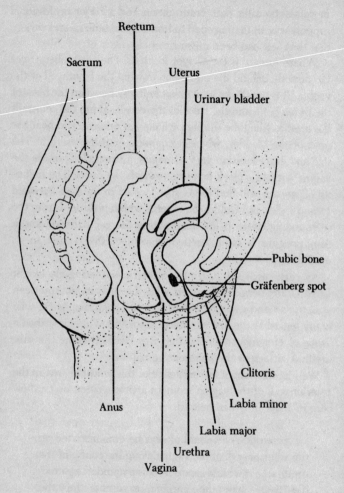

Illustration 1
The Gräfenberg Spot (Internal Female Genitalia)

felt. It swells out greatly at the end of orgasm. The most stimulating part is located at the posterior urethra, where it arises from the neck of the bladder.[2,3]

Gräfenberg suggested how important this area can be, because "the female partner is always aware [when] the finger or the penis loses contact with the vaginal part of the urethra, and she adjusts herself to this by changing her position."[4]

The significance of Gräfenberg's observations is not obvious unless we recall that in the 1940s there was a major scientific controversy over the focal point of female sexual arousal. Freud's radical ideas had become popular in America, and professionals were beginning to take sides on the question of clitoral vs. vaginal orgasm. Researchers hoped to settle the controversy by identifying the anatomical sites of sexual arousal.

The sexual significance of the clitoris was relatively easy to establish, since the organ is so accessible. Kinsey found it sensitive to touch in 98 percent of his subjects. The physiological sensation of the vagina was more difficult to ascertain for many reasons. Although 90 percent of his subjects found the vagina sensitive to deep pressure, only approximately 12 percent found the vagina sensitive to gentle touch. Kinsey concluded that:

> . . . in most females the walls of the vagina are devoid of end organs of touch and are quite insensitive when they are gently stroked or lightly pressed . . . most of those who did make some response had the sensitivity confined to a certain point, in most cases on the upper [anterior] wall of the vagina just inside the vaginal entrance.[5]

In spite of this data, Kinsey chose to assume that sexual arousal had to have a single focus, and since he believed that the clitoris is the homologue of the male penis, he therefore identified it as the area of sexual sensitivity in the female. Gräfenberg did not dispute Kinsey's findings about the clitoris, but he did insist that the vagina was also important. Because of his clear descriptions of the relationship of a sensitive area in the vagina to sexual pleasure, Perry and Whipple named this area the Gräfenberg spot.

Research about women and their sexual response is a relatively new area of investigation, largely because of our culture's inherited presumption that women are passive receptors of male sexual activity and as such do not (and should not) have the desire or the capacity to respond as sexual beings. For many years it was (and in many places still is) believed that the sole purpose of sexual intercourse is procreation and that woman's role is to conceive and bear children, not to enjoy sexuality.

A thirty-five-year-old woman who has been married for fourteen years said this about the study of female sexual response:

> It seems incredible that this is only now being studied. One has to wonder if discrimination against women has somehow come into play, historically speaking. It is entirely possible that much more research would have been done about this subject if most of the researchers weren't men. And isn't it pathetic that it's 1982 and we women are just beginning to discuss this subject?

With clear insight about the ways in which the second-class status of women diminished the amount of attention paid to their sexual problems by the male-dominated medical profession, in 1953, Gräfenberg commented, "The undervaluation of female secrets went so far that even the meaning of orgasm and the localization of the erotic zones were not exactly recognized."[6]

He further believed that:

> The location of the erogenic zone on the anterior wall of the vagina proves that the human animal is built in the same manner as the other quadrupeds. In probably the most commonly adopted position in human intercourse in the Western world, where the female is on her back, the thrust of the penis does not reach the urethral part of the vagina, unless the angle of the erect penis is very steep, or the legs of the female partner are placed over the shoulders of the male partner. I agree with LeMon Clark that man is designed as a quadruped and therefore the normal position would be intercourse *a posteriori* [in which the man enters the vagina from behind].[7]

Elaine Morgan, writing in 1972, also described the area of the G spot, although she does not call it that. In *The Descent of Woman*, she wrote:

> What triggers it off [orgasm] is a brief but vigorous application of rapid rhythmical friction. . . . The desired friction is applied, usually from behind, to the interior wall of the vagina. . . . The only other point we need note here is that in many primates and other quadrupeds the pressure comes not only from

behind, but from above downward, so that it is applied to the *ventral* [front] wall of the vagina.[8]

It is well known that almost all mammals copulate in the rear-entry position.

The remainder of Morgan's thesis, that the mechanism in the *human* female became somewhat atrophied because of her evolutionary and cultural history, is controversial, but this may account for the fact that some women report difficulty in reaching the G spot while others are concerned about positioning themselves correctly, depending upon the particular physical attributes of their partners.

Although Morgan approached the subject from an entirely different vantage point, through her study of ethology, evolution, and anthropology, she arrived at conclusions remarkably similar to those of Gräfenberg, who was primarily a practicing physician. She wrote that vigorous thrusting through rear-entry is the optimal position for sexual satisfaction in all female mammals, including women.

Many of the women and men we have interviewed or who have written to us confirm Gräfenberg's and Morgan's statements. For example, a forty-year-old singer from Mexico said:

> *I never thought the clitoris was important. I don't like to have it touched, and I don't touch it myself. When I took a course in women's studies, I got very angry because all the women there emphasized the clitoris. For me it is a very poor place. My best orgasms come when the man enters me from behind. Then I can guide him to the right place and help him to touch the exact spot inside me.*

Angela, a fifty-six-year-old architect, brought up so strictly that she had never been kissed before she went to college, said "It takes a good-size penis to hit the spot in the missionary position. I need the man to penetrate further. Rear-entry is a much more satisfying position."

We told a friend about this. In her mid-thirties, a professor and an ardent feminist, she was incensed, because rear-entry "puts the woman in an inferior position." Whether one regards the position as "inferior" or "enjoyable" is a highly subjective matter. There is nothing innately inferior or superior about such a preference. What is important is that we recognize that different women have different needs, that a variety of options should be available, and that women should actively participate in the choice of sexual positions and activities.

A fifty-six-year-old life insurance salesman talked about a woman he had had sex with in his early thirties. The woman, he said,

> . . . *was absolutely wonderful to be with. She had a unique way of making love. She would caress me all over, and when my erection was huge and strong, she would back up and insert my penis in her vagina from the rear. She would position us very carefully and then move vigorously, saying that she wanted a lot of pressure on exactly the right spot.*

Not only does the position for intercourse have some bearing on stimulation of the G spot, but the physical makeup and cooperation of the partners are also extremely important. Gräfenberg told us more about the role of the partner: "The angle which the penis forms with the body has an important significance and has to be taken into consideration. It may be that the fame of the 'perfect lover' is based on such physiological characteristics."[9]

April, forty-two, and married for the second time, confirms that statement:

> *It is a different experience than I ever had before. With Dan, we can lie facing each other and his penis reaches that spot in my vagina which feels so wonderful and which always brings me to orgasm. I think it's because of the way his penis lies when it is erect, flat against his tummy. It was never that way with my other partners.*

Other couples report that intercourse with the female on top is the best position for stimulating the area of the G spot. Some report that a smaller penis is sometimes more effective than a larger penis in this position. As the thirty-year-old wife of a physician wrote:

> *I have always had orgasms, but I have never had much stimulation when the penis was completely inside my vagina. In fact, sometimes my excitement and arousal would end abruptly when the penis entered me completely. I have always been most excitable when the penis was only one-half or one-third its way into my vagina. Now I know why—at that point it hit my "magic spot."*

Another woman who has been married thirty-three years reported that:

> *I must tell you that you are dead right about the Gräfenberg spot. I hadn't known what it was called,*

but it is definitely there. I have heard so many sex experts mislead too many poor women into thinking that clitoral stimulation was orgasm—of course, that feels good—but nothing compares with the real orgasm, which occurs deeply in the vagina, and if you can manage to get both at the same time, it is rapture indeed.

Nevertheless, some find that the G spot can be reached in the predominant male-on-top position, commonly called "the missionary position." As a woman who has been married twenty years wrote:

While intercourse from the rear or when I am on top makes this spot more accessible, I find that it works fine in the missionary position if deep penetration is made possible, and if his erection swells, particularly before ejaculation.

A Muslim from Iran reported that in his culture men are taught how to please their mates through stimulation of a special place. Asked if he was talking about the clitoris, he said, "No, it's something inside a woman, and she enjoys it more when she is on top." His wife says he is absolutely right and when he is on top of her it isn't as satisfying.

Knowledge of sexuality and sexual techniques is more cultural than instinctive. Cultures less sexually repressive than our own celebrate the existence of female orgasm and teach their members methods of achieving it. In such cultures female orgasm is the expected state of affairs. During the First World War, anthropologist Bronislaw Malinowski lived with one such group, the Trobriand Islanders. Some of the cat's-cradle-type string games played by the Trobrianders were explicitly sexual.

One showed two loops, representing two foci of erotic arousal. (The game was played by moving the fingers first in one and then in the other of the loops, producing a movement that causes each loop in turn to vibrate rapidly.) Malinowski interpreted this as symbolizing two clitorises, saying: "There is obviously a little anatomical inaccuracy in this arrangement, since in nature there is only one organ and in this the clitoris is placed at the top and not at the bottom of the vulva."[10] He was not able to conceive of two centers of erotic arousal in women. With the advantage of hindsight, it seems almost certain that the string game represented not two clitorises but the clitoris and the G spot.

Another woman wrote from Panama: "We are quite conscious of the 'Gräfenberg Spot.' It is called here 'La Bella Loca.' I knew of it from when I was about fifteen years old. I am now sixty-five years old. We are a nation of sex-loving people."

The G spot is probably composed of a complex network of blood vessels, the paraurethral glands and ducts, nerve endings, and the tissue surrounding the bladder neck. In those woman examined by us (or by others and reported to us), this sensitive area swelled with stimulation and the soft tissue began to feel hard, with well defined edges. Under conditions favorable to sexual arousal, the swelling takes place very rapidly. The cellular structure of the G spot is, at this time, unknown. Researchers at several medical schools are currently attempting to identify the exact nature of the tissues that compose it.

One controversial question is whether the G spot can be considered a homologue of the male prostate. This controversy goes back to ancient Rome, where Galen, a physician writing in the second century A.D., raised the question and voted yes. But William Masters, commenting on the Perry and Whipple research in April 1981, insisted that the word *prostate* is not appropriate.[11]

We tend to believe that the area of the G spot includes a vestigial homologue of the male prostate, despite the fact that many physicians state that it has no known urological or gynecological function. A significant difference between the two is that the male prostate gland is more highly defined and more uniform in size, shape, and location than the G spot. Nevertheless, women and men may be more anatomically alike than was previously conceded.

An article in *The New York Times* in October 1980 told the story of a father who successfully breast-fed his daughter for eight months. He was able to do this by taking estrogen and following the procedures used by women throughout the world when they want to breast-feed infants even though they have not recently been pregnant. The method requires that the infant first suckle extensively, since stimulation of the nipples eventually initiates the lactation process. Simultaneously with suckling, milk is introduced into the baby's mouth through an eye dropper until the milk flow from the father's nipples is firmly established. Whether many men could do this is not known. Motivation and persistence are key factors even in the case of women who want to breast-feed without bearing a child. But if even only a small percentage of men can breast-feed, perhaps the G spot can function in a manner similar to the male prostate.

To discover whether the G spot does in fact exist in all women, Perry and Whipple had a physician or nurse examine more than 400 women who had volunteered to be research subjects. The G spot was found in each of the women examined. Although we cannot yet state with certainty that every woman has one, more and more physicians are now reporting that they are finding the G spot.

If the G spot is uniformly found when sought, why has it been overlooked until now? Many people assume that physicians should know everything about the human body. However, they are taught to avoid procedures that might cause their patients to feel sexually aroused. During the course of a normal gynecological examination, the area of the G spot is usually palpated, but not stimulated. It is easy, therefore, to understand why the G spot has been overlooked. In its unstimulated state, it is relatively small and difficult to locate, especially since you can't see it. Just as the penis does not usually swell during the course of a medical exam, neither does the G spot. On the basis of office knowledge alone, physicians would be forced to conclude that the average male penis is flaccid and approximately two inches in length!

In *A New View of a Woman's Body*, compiled by the Federation of Feminist Women's Health Centers, the area we call the G spot is called the "urethral sponge." The authors were unable to find this structure mentioned in medical textbooks, so they named it themselves.[12] They explain that it surrounds and protects the urethra by filling with blood during sexual excitement and intercourse, acting as a buffer between the penis and the urethra.

How can a woman find her own G spot? It is almost impossible if you are lying on your back, because gravity tends to pull the internal organs down and away from the vaginal entrance, so one would need very long fingers and a short vagina. A sitting or squatting position would be better. Because the first sensation women usually experience when the G spot is stimulated feels very much like an urgent need to urinate, one solution is to look for the spot while seated on the toilet. Urinate before attempting to locate your G spot so you will not worry that your activities are signaling a full bladder. Explore the upper front wall of your vagina by applying firm upward pressure. (Some women find it helpful to apply simultaneous downward pressure with the other hand on the outside of the abdomen just above the pubic bone.) As you stimulate the G spot and it begins to swell, it can often be felt as a small lump between the two sets of fingers. You will probably experience a distinct internal sensation that will cease when you release the finger pressure.

For physicians attempting to locate the G spot with the patient lying on her back, this bimanual method of examination is also a good one. Feedback from the patient when using this method helps the inexperienced health practitioner to locate the spot more easily. Zwi Hoch, M.D., of Israel, also uses the bimanual technique to teach patients and their partners how to find the area.[13]

To the finger, the G spot feels like a small bean, and, when stimulated, it may swell to the size of a dime or sometimes becomes as large as a half-dollar. Some women have larger spots, just as some women have larger breasts and some men have larger penises. The size of any of these body parts in no way affects their responsiveness to stimulation. Women vary in their enjoyment of G spot stimulation in the same way that some women enjoy stimulation of their nipples more than others. Physical examination has revealed that the G spot is often smaller in postmenopausal women, yet response to stimulation seems no different from the responses of women who are not menopausal.

If you continue stroking the area with a firm touch, which should feel slightly to moderately pleasurable, you may notice twinges or contractions in your uterus. Experiment with your G spot as you may have done with your clitoris, if and when you learned to masturbate that way. You will probably want a heavier pressure on the G spot and will feel the sensation deeper inside than you do when you masturbate clitorally.

As you progress beyond the feeling of a full bladder, you may want to move to a bed or other more comfortable location. If you are still concerned about urinating, take a towel with you. Continue stimulating the spot while kneeling or sitting on your feet with your knees apart. Should you experience an orgasm, notice if and how it differs from the ones you enjoy through clitoral stimulation. Some women will ejaculate a clear fluid when they have this type of orgasm. If you are among them, you may again feel as if you need to urinate just before this happens. (If you do ejaculate, the fluid will be much clearer and whiter than urine and will not smell like it. See chapter 3 for a more complete discussion of female ejaculation.)

If you have a partner with whom you feel comfortable, you may want to share the discovery of your G spot. You may find this easier if you are lying on your belly, legs apart and hips rotated slightly upwards. Have your partner insert two fingers (palm down) and explore the front wall of your vagina (which will be closest to the bed), with a firm touch. Move your pelvis to facilitate contact with the G spot. Tell your partner what feels good. This position is also an excellent one for stimulation by the penis. If your partner inserts one or two fingers (palm up) into your vagina while you are lying on your back, the G spot can usually be felt by putting pressure against the top wall of the vagina, in an area about halfway between the back of the pubic bone and the end of the vagina where the cervix is located. Putting a second hand on top of the abdomen, just above the pubic hairline with a downward pressure, sometimes helps to stimulate the G spot.

Another position favorable for many couples is with the man lying on his back and the woman sitting with his erect penis in her vagina. This allows the woman to move in such a way as to bring the penis into contact with her G spot, and may also lead to multiple orgasms. Don't be surprised if the first time you experiment with this position you experience nothing or only mild pleasure. It may take practice, sometimes several sessions, to learn this new technique. If you don't find it pleasurable at first, or if it becomes irritating, stop. Try another time. If or when you experience pleasure, you may want to continue.

As noted earlier, the proximity of the G spot to the bladder and the urethra often makes women feel that they have to urinate—even when stimulation of the G spot does not result in ejaculation. This, in turn, may have more serious consequences, causing many women to suppress their feelings at this point or even to refrain from sexual activity because they feel ashamed, embarrassed, or fear that they may actually urinate. By blocking these feelings, they also block and prevent orgasm.

> *Barbara, a twenty-seven-year-old seamstress with a history of bed-wetting as a young child, came for marriage counseling. Although not her reason for seeking help, one difficulty she experienced, which infuriated her husband, was that every time they started to have intercourse, she would get up to urinate in spite of the fact that she always took care to urinate before commencing any sexual activity. Her fears were compounded because of her early history of bed-wetting. Reassured by the information that such a feeling is common but does not mean she is really going to urinate, this young woman was able to accept these sensations for what they were and go on to experience uninterrupted intercourse and a pleasurable release.*

Although many women prefer gentle stimulation of the clitoris, pleasurable stimulation of the G spot often requires very firm to strong pressure. As indicated earlier, once a woman has discovered her G spot, learned how it feels and where it is located, she may be able to stimulate the spot herself by using external pressure on the abdomen, slightly above the pubic bone. Said Virginia, twenty-four, a trainer of seeing-eye dogs:

> At first I didn't know anything about the G spot. All my sensations had been confined to my clitoris. But after working to strengthen the muscles in my vagina, I began to reach orgasm with my husband, particularly when he entered me from behind. He is often away on business, and so now I've learned to masturbate by stimulating the G spot through my tummy. Touching my G spot with one hand and my clitoris with the other is no substitute for being with him, but it is certainly a lovely way to masturbate.

The sensitivity of the G spot may account for some of the orgasmic sensations reported by women during childbirth, for it is possible that the G spot may be stimulated during the baby's progress down the birth canal.

One woman wrote:

> I recently gave birth to my second child. Is it possible that the pushing effect you mentioned in connection with G spot stimulation might be related to the involuntary pushing urge during the final stages of labor? It appears that the G spot would have considerable pressure exerted upon it as the baby's presenting part reached the pubic bone.

A woman of sixty-one, married for thirty-seven years, said:

I have given birth to three children, alive, well, and happy. However, one experience I've had really bothered me. When I was having my second child, I was in the hospital and the doctor told me to go to the bathroom. On the toilet I had the most terrific orgasm ever. Sex was far from my mind. The doctor either didn't care to talk about it, or didn't believe me. I've always been made to feel guilty about it and close women friends have looked at me like I was crazy. Could the position of the fetus have put pressure on the G spot?

This is certainly an area worthy of further investigation.

Having a highly responsive G spot can occasionally be a problem, as it was for the woman who provided the following communication:

I am a woman whose Gräfenberg spot is very prominent and sensitive. I enjoy sex to the maximum because of it. But I have problems getting through a gynecological exam because the speculum presses on the spot and I instantly begin to climax. I must concentrate very hard to prevent it.

This was confirmed by one man who wrote:

I discovered the "Gräfenberg Spot" many years ago quite by accident. I didn't know what it was, but I knew that it almost made my partner come unglued when I touched it just right. I've had the pleasure of engaging in sexual intercourse with several different women during the past years, and I've noticed that stimulation of that spot gets a different response in each woman from weak to "volcanic."

The existence and location of the G spot is extremely important for surgeons to consider when performing operations. Cutting in the wrong place may deprive certain women of future sexual pleasure. From conversations and letters we have exchanged, it seems that surgery can have both positive and negative effects on sexuality, and this may depend upon the type of surgery performed as well as which nerves and tissues were disturbed. Some women, for instance, report an increase in pleasurable feelings after removal of the uterus.

I've always felt an orgasm from that spot. It feels great, and my hubby and I love it. Nine years ago, when I was thirty, I had to have a hysterectomy. I still have my ovaries, however, and I feel it more since I had the operation.

On the other hand, some women report the opposite effect:

I have been quite concerned for some time and asked the doctor who performed my hysterectomy why I can't have an inside climax anymore like I experienced before surgery. He laughed it off and said there is no such thing. He had also done a bladder repair. Could that have had anything to do with my inability to reach a climax as before? Is there any corrective surgery that can now be done?

Since we can no longer assume that the clitoris is the major source of erotic pleasure for all women, disturbing any tissue in the area may disrupt or eliminate the G spot, thus diminishing or even eliminating an important source of sexual pleasure. One woman asked:

> *I do have a very important question that has been troubling me since my gynecologist told me this past June that I needed a partial hysterectomy. I am forty-two years old, and for all of my twenty-two years of married life, my sex life has been very fulfilling. I experience the deep orgasms described as a pushing down of the uterus, and that is what bothers me. How can the sensation possibly be the same if there is no uterus? Needless to say, I have been reluctant to discuss this aspect of my worries with my gynecologist, who is, by the way, a man. And though I have a great deal of confidence in my doctor, I alone know how my body feels and responds during orgasm, and I am afraid that anything a man might tell me in this matter would not carry too much weight.*

Gräfenberg did note that a woman may be unable to experience orgasm after a hysterectomy "if the erotogenic zone of the anterior vaginal wall was removed at the time of the operation."[14] Yet many women who have had hysterectomies report that they continue to experience the "deep orgasms" accompanied by the pushing-down sensation, even though they no longer have their uterus. One explanation for this may be that the nerves supplying the uterus and the G spot are still intact, and thus the muscular response in the upper part of the vagina is not affected.

Another important medical concern is the effect of the diaphragm on the G spot. The diaphragm, a method of birth control often recommended in the United States, may block stimulation of the G spot. In some cases, it is difficult if not impossible to feel the G spot with a diaphragm in place. A young woman, who felt guilty and embarrassed about the intensity of her sexual response, told us:

> It was frightening. My reaction to intercourse was such a strong one, and we were not prepared for it by anything we had been taught. When I first started having intercourse, I would come and come. Then I got fitted for a diaphragm and, thank God, that didn't happen anymore.

One woman wrote:

> I am a twenty-nine-year-old married woman who has been experiencing this sensation for ten years, and wouldn't trade it for the world. There was a short time when I used a diaphragm and noticed right off it was next to impossible to reach the peak of this sensation.

But for other women, the use of a diaphragm has not interfered with stimulation of the G spot. This forty-one-year-old woman, married for twenty-three years, reported, "I have been using a diaphragm for five years now, and it does not seem to hinder the orgasmic experience and sometimes enhances it. But positioning is important, and not only back entry—it will also occur with legs highly elevated."

It may be that the fit of the diaphragm in relation to the location of the G spot in each woman is important and should be carefully taken into consideration when deciding which method of birth control to practice. For women whose spot is located right behind the pubic bone (as compared to farther up in the vagina), the diaphragm is less likely to interfere with orgasmic response. In instances where the diaphragm does interfere with sensation, one answer may be the use of the cervical cap, although it has not yet been approved by the Food and Drug Administration and is now only available experimentally in the United States. The cap fits directly over the cervix and does not interfere with stimulation of the G spot. Gräfenberg and Dickinson were aware of this as early as 1944 when they wrote:

> Occasionally, a patient has reported failure to reach orgasm when wearing a vaginal diaphragm, due to the principal or only zone of erogenous feeling being located along the suburethral surface of the anterior vaginal wall. Because the cervix cap leaves the anterior wall uncovered, whereas the diaphragm covers it, these patients can obtain orgasm after the change is made.[15]

Women who are happy with the diaphragm as their form of birth control, even though it may impair stimulation of the G spot during intercourse, may want to experiment with stimulation of the spot with a partner's finger before inserting the diaphragm.

Men also have a pleasurable area located, like the G spot, around the urethra at the neck of the bladder. It is known as the prostate gland. Like the G spot, it can be pleasurably stimulated with a finger or penis, but is not easy for a man to reach by himself.

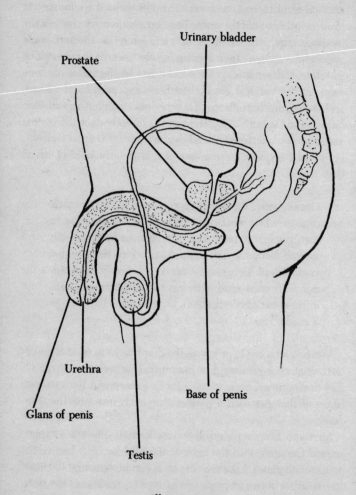

Illustration 2
Male Genitalia

Some men overcome the problem by inserting their thumb and pressing against the anterior (front) rectal wall, massaging downward towards the anus. The best position for this is lying on one's back with the knees up and feet flat on the bed. Some men prefer to draw their legs up farther towards the chest. The prostate can be felt as a soft mass a few inches inside the rectum on the anterior wall. (Most medical authorities recommend that one never insert anything into the rectum and then bring it in contact with other parts of the body without first thoroughly washing with soap and water.)

Initially, massage of the prostate, like stimulation of the G spot, is sometimes perceived as unpleasant, particularly when the purpose is a medical examination. But when the prostate is massaged as part of a sexual encounter, men report that the sensation is pleasurable. When the correct area is touched, an unusual and good feeling, quite different emotionally and physiologically from the one normally associated with stimulation of the glans (tip of the penis), follows. This parallels the difference women report between stimulation of the G spot and stimulation of the clitoris.

When the prostate is stimulated in this fashion to the point of ejaculation, the fluid usually flows out rather than spurts, although the amount is comparable to that of a normal ejaculation. Men report that the orgasm they experience as a result of stimulation of the prostate gland is more like the pushing-down feeling reported by women in connection with the stimulation of the G spot. You will recall that the Hoyts, whose experience was discussed at the start of this chapter, experimented happily with this type of activity.

Our understanding about the pleasurable aspects of the male prostate has been enhanced by our new knowledge of the pleasurable aspects of the G spot. The first person to describe the G spot in detail was, in fact, not Gräfenberg, but a seventeenth-century Dutch anatomist Regnier de Graaf, who provided the first modern descriptions of the human male and female genitalia. Unlike several contemporary anatomists, he considered the erotic as well as the structural significance of the female sexual organs. De Graaf described the membranous lining of the urethra in detail, saying that "the substance could be called quite aptly the female prostatae or corpus glandulosum . . . " He continues: "The function of the 'prostatae' is to generate a pituitoserous juice which makes women more libidinous. . . . Here too it should be noted that the discharge from the female prostatae causes as much pleasure as does that from the male prostatae."[16]

De Graaf's work first came to our attention through Sevely and Bennett's article in the February 1978 issue of the *Journal of Sex Research*. It was their excellent review, analyzing the literature about female ejaculation, that ignited the spark for much of the research with which this book is concerned.

Knowledge about the G spot was not, by any means, limited to the writings of de Graaf and Gräfenberg. Many other physicians and anatomists have described it—not, however, as the seat of pleasure but as a potential site of venereal infection or surgical complications. The function of the G spot in health was of little or no concern.[17]

Alexander Skene, M.D., a physician writing in 1880, was concerned with the problem of draining the various glands and ducts surrounding the female urethra when they became infected with gonococcus. Skene drew diagrams to facilitate this process, and to this day, the female urethral glands are known as Skene's glands. A number of other researchers began writing about these glands shortly therafter. They reported that embryologically the urethral glands of the female could be considered homologous to the male prostatic glands, and that the glands have a structure similar to the prostatic gland of a five- to six-month-old male fetus.[18]

In 1941 George Caldwell, M.D., reported that the glands vary in the extent of their development in different individuals.

> They possess a structure and elaborate a secretion comparable only to the prostatic glands of the male . . . they are embryonic remnants which may have no essential function in the female, but which are apparently capable of some response to functional stimuli in the normal female, as indicated by the frequent occurrence of retained secretion within the glands.[19]

For close to half a century, no one else had considered Skene's findings worthy of further attention. Then, in 1943, obstetrician and gynecologist John W. Huffman, M.D., began investigating Skene's glands and concluded that Skene himself had underestimated, by a good deal, the extent of the glands and ducts surrounding the urethra.[20] That same year an article in the *Journal of the American Medical Association* reported cases of hypertrophy or enlargement of the "prostate" gland in females that had to be treated by surgery.[21,22]

In 1953, urologist Samuel Berkow, M.D., concluded that this tissue is erectile and can be viewed as a "corpus spongeosum"[23] (like the erectile tissue in the male penis). But Berkow never studied the conditions under which it might become erect. His interest was in urination and he felt that the function of this "erectile tissue" was to pinch off the urethra and thus control urination. Unfortunately, other urologists failed to find this sphincteric function, and quickly forgot that the "erectile tissue" might have other purposes outside the domain of their own discipline.[24]

Shall we refer to this cluster of tissue as the "female prostate gland"? There is no argument about its anatomical and embryological similarity; the question seems to be merely one of semantics. One function of the male prostate is to manufacture part of the seminal fluid. (The sperm is added by the testicles.) If the G spot or the tissue in close proximity to it is a homologue of the male prostate, then it should not surprise us (although this has not yet been validated scientifically and remains at this time a hypothesis) that it may in some women, and under some circumstances, also generate a fluid—which brings us to the second rediscovery that Perry and Whipple called to the attention of the sex researchers, female ejaculation.

·3·

Female Ejaculation

In May of 1981, *Newsweek* published an article entitled "Just How the Sexes Differ." One of the items listed under the heading "clear-cut differences," along with lactation in women, was ejaculation in men. *Newsweek* was wrong on both counts. We have already mentioned in the preceding chapter that under special circumstances men can breast-feed. We also know that many women report that they ejaculate. In fact, knowledge about female ejaculation is ancient history.

As we mentioned earlier, Aristotle was probably the first to write about female ejaculation, and Galen is said to have known about it in the second century A.D. De Graaf, in his *New Treatise Concerning the Generative Organs of Women*, described the female prostate in some detail. He noted that ". . . during the sexual act it discharges to lubricate the tract so copiously that it even flows outside the pudenda. This is the matter which may have been taken to be actual female semen."[1] De Graaf also described the fluid as "rushing out," with "impetus" and "in one gush."

Although female ejaculation is a more spectacular and controversial finding than the G spot, it is a phenomenon that apparently occurs in fewer women, at least in our culture. All of the women examined by Perry and Whipple and their colleagues had a G spot, although before the examination many were unaware of its existence. Several years ago, when we began asking coed audiences whether they had ever personally experienced or encountered female ejaculation, only about 10 percent raised their hands. This percentage has been steadily increasing and recently the response has been closer to 40 percent. How can we account for such a change? Recognizing the existence of female ejaculation may help women to identify and articulate their own experiences more precisely. Knowing that some women have ejaculated may help other women and their partners feel more comfortable about admitting that they too have experienced this. Or perhaps more women are actually allowing it to happen for the first time. On the other hand, maybe other women are highly suggestible, or are just giving the new socially acceptable answer; however, the percentage of women who claim to ejaculate is highest when they respond anonymously.

Even though ejaculation may not occur in the majority of women, the topic is a very important one. Consider, for example, the problem of this couple:

When Lisa opened her eyes, it was not yet dawn. John, her husband of two years, lay beside her, his arm resting gently across her bare thigh. Was it his touch that had triggered her erotic dream? Thank goodness, she thought, I managed to wake up before reaching a climax. To reassure herself, she reached beneath her bare skin to check the sheets. Finding them dry, she sighed and turned her head to look at John. Few men had ever attracted her so deeply. No one she had ever known had been as gentle or as kind or had had such deep emotional or sexual feelings towards her. And therein lay her problem. So different from the anorgasmic women she knew, Lisa had no trouble coming. On the contrary, from experiences she had had before marriage, she knew that she was multi-orgasmic, capable of powerful responses that filled her with incredible happiness But that was something of the past. She could not allow herself to let go like that with John, because when she did something terribly embarrassing happened. Every time she had had an ecstatic experience, she had urinated. It was as though the two experiences were inextricably linked. She felt deeply ashamed. With a sexual problem like that, who would want her?

Lisa met John after she had had a series of unsatisfying relationships. The attraction between them was strong and immediate, but Lisa decided not to allow any physical intimacy. She cared too much to risk losing him. Instead of telling him she was a virgin, she explained her diffidence in another way. She maintained that by allowing a sexual relationship to develop too quickly, they might forfeit any chance to have the true friendship necessary for a lasting love. John was tired of the singles scene, tired of swinging from one bed to another, tired of sexual encounters that ended as quickly as they had started. His attraction to Lisa was much more than physical, so he decided to be patient and wait until she was comfortable with him. At the time, he was not interested in marriage, and there were moments when he wondered whether Lisa was using this as a ploy to force him down the aisle.

Even so, John loved Lisa and was finally happy to take his vows. Marriage gave Lisa a strong sense of security. Now she would allow herself a full sexual life without fear that John would leave her because of her peculiar sexual aberration. But when the wedding night came, Lisa felt she had better hold back. She loved John too much to risk his disapproval. So she managed to keep herself from surrendering to John's wonderful lovemaking. From that day on, she began to fake climax. It was the one lie she told him, the only secret between them.

Lisa shifted her body to a more comfortable position. Turning away from her husband, she instinctively felt for her clitoris. Her vagina was damp, and she began to pleasure herself and wanted to sigh out loud as her excitement mounted, but she pushed her face deeper into the pillow instead, fearful of waking her husband.

How many times had she done this? she asked herself. How many times had she turned away from John as he lay beside her, and masturbated to climax? She was convinced it was something she should not do now that she was happily married. The Church had told her so, and she also remembered reading, in a course at college, what Freud had said about women who rely on their clitorises for pleasure. She knew she could respond during intercourse, but that would only bring on the symptom that filled her with shame. And she had never read anything about that, either, in college or afterward. It also puzzled her that clitoral climax should be considered childish, since she knew she could derive gratification from both intercourse and mas-turbation.

Deep in pleasure, she turned her head to make sure that John was still safely asleep and discovered that his eyes were wide open. Wrapping his arms around her, he drew her closer.

"Do you know how long I've been lying here wanting you?" he said. A look of longing came over his face.

"Please, John," she said, "not now." Jolted, he sat up, his brow furrowed with confusion.

"I just don't understand you. You can't expect me to believe that you're not excited. There's no way on earth you can expect me to believe that."

He got up and started to dress. "You know, Lisa, we shouldn't go on like this without at least talking about it. I love you dearly. I couldn't have found a better wife anywhere. You're a beautiful woman. You're really good for me, and yet you're afraid to really enjoy sex with me."

"But I come with you all the time. You know that."

"That's what you've been telling me for the past two years. But I know differently. Do you really think you can fool me like that indefinitely? Don't you know I can tell what's going on?"

"If you knew it all this time, why didn't you ever say anything?"

"Then you admit it, you admit that you've been faking?"

Lisa looked away, refusing to say another word. Perhaps John would suggest a visit to her gynecol-

ogist. She had already been that route. When she consulted her gynecologist, before she had even met John, he had referred her to a psychiatrist who, in the twenty sessions she attended, began probing into her childhood patterns. Had she been a bed-wetter? What kind of toilet training had she been subjected to? The inquiries led nowhere and left Lisa feeling like a freak.

Lisa and John are not unique. We've received letters from many men and women (many of them "closet" ejaculators) whose relationships have been upset because of female ejaculation. A thirty-four-year-old woman wrote:

I couldn't have relations with my husband without wetting the bed, at least a little. My husband was no help, he kept telling me to go to the bathroom before I came to bed. After a divorce and change of partner, I was mortified when my new man also accused me of urinating on him.

The author of a book about sex told us:

I am reminded of the story of a friend of mine, whose boyfriend was so totally disgusted by her "urinating" during orgasms that he left her. The poor girl spent a very long time recovering from that wound. She thought there was something wrong with her and was told by her physician that it was a physiological problem, that many women lose control of their bladders during orgasm, so she avoided sexual contact for years, and spent many dollars and hours on psychological counseling.

Fortunately, not everyone was so adversely affected. We received as many letters from people who told us that their relationship was enhanced by female ejaculation. One woman wrote:

> *I've experienced "female ejaculation" since my first sexual encounter at fifteen. Since sexuality was not discussed back then, I only had to assume that all women experienced what I did. I achieved orgasm like that, strictly through fondling and petting with my boyfriend using his middle finger to penetrate deep enough. (He had long fingers—I know because since then I've been with four other lovers and not all of them proved as stimulating.) I literally soaked my pants if we did it in his car and, don't laugh, I used to dry them in the Laundromat before I went home.*
>
> *Not until recently did I realize I was fairly unique in what I was experiencing. Talking about sexual matters became more open and I have described what I experienced to my sisters, friends, and even my mom within the last year. Not a one knew what I was talking about.*
>
> *I finally asked my ob/gyn where all this liquid is stored. He said, "What liquid?" After I told him what happens with me, he told me it was urine, and I felt like belting the old coot over the head because he was so obstinate. He said the vaginal wall secretes some amount of juices, but nothing like I was describing.*

She was not convinced by his explanation and concluded that she has a sort of "gift" sexually.

Here is what another of the more fortunate women said:

> I first experienced sexual encounters at the time of
> my marriage, my husband being my first and only
> partner. From the very beginning I have always felt
> that pushing-forward-and-out feeling, and almost
> always had some sort of discharge with it. But it
> wasn't until recently (after the birth of my second
> child) that my so-called spot actually became
> noticed. Whenever sexually excited this spot begins
> to swell to the point of protruding, where it actually
> comes out to reach my husband's penis. My dis-
> charge is always in the amount of or more than that
> of my husband's ejaculation. There have been times
> where my husband can recall it coming in such a
> force that it actually squirts his abdomen.
>
> My sexual life is very, very fulfilling and satisfy-
> ing.

With women, as with men, ejaculation involves the ejection
of fluid in gushes through the urethra at the moment of orgasm.
The phenomenon seems to occur more frequently in women
when the G spot is stimulated.

One woman from Texas, married for twenty-eight years,
reported, "I have had this happening since 1974. This liquid
does not expel during foreplay or clitoral orgasms, only when
this spot is massaged, either by the penis or the finger. I am
forty-eight years old. Life began at forty I guess."

One man wrote:

> When I perform oral sex on my wife, I insert one
> finger into her vagina and push upward. I can feel
> her swell and swell until the fluid begins to flow. I

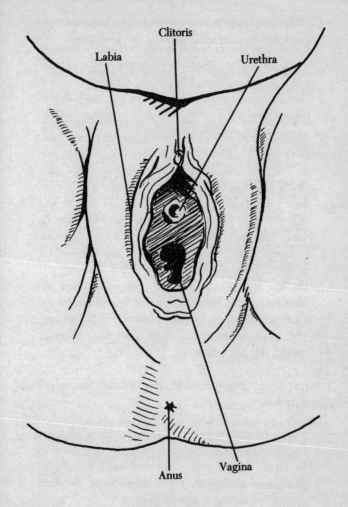

Illustration 3
External Female Genitalia

call it love juice. It is something like a double table-spoonful. She has an orgasm as the juice flows.

Another woman wrote that she had had a good sex life with her husband but didn't achieve orgasm at first.

We were married in 1969 when it was still too early for women to enjoy sex. I was happy to have a husband who loved me so much that I didn't care one way or the other about orgasm for me. Well, one day something happened! My husband was stimulating me orally and had a finger or two in my vagina. My God! Something in there was doing something. Boy, did that feel good. All of a sudden out gushed this liquid. I thought I had urinated by accident from the stimulation. From that day on, this has been happening. For twelve years now we have had a very happy life, sexually and otherwise. I am sure that part of that is because of this discovery. Lovemaking is so much fun, but certainly messy. We don't care.

A few women report that they also ejaculate through clitoral stimulation alone:

I use a vibrator regularly. During a clitoral orgasm, I noticed a sudden discharge of fluid. I thought it to be urine, but on closer examination, I found this fluid to be similar to, if not the same as, the fluid ejaculated during a vaginal orgasm.

The amount of ejected fluid seems in general to vary from woman to woman and, in individual cases, may also vary from one occasion to the next. A fifty-six-year-old man informed us that "... my experience has been that the amount varies. I would say one-half a cup to one cup is common if the man keeps working at it, and these orgasms are always the best for the woman." A twenty-three-year-old systems analyst wrote:

> *I was definitely aware of the pushing of my uterus towards the front and the intensity of the orgasm(s) I experienced brought tears to my eyes. But I was unaware of the tremendous amount of fluid produced until I got up from the bed, which was sopping wet. "I did that?" I asked him. "Yep." "All of it?" "Well, I haven't even taken my pants off yet." "Wow," I said. After that, my Gräfenberg spot became my "Love Button," and my appreciation of sex increased twofold with the discovery that I can "come like a man."*

A woman of sixty, three times a grandmother, told us, "Since the first year of our marriage, I have expelled copious amounts of fluid. Sometimes it is only a few drops, but at other times it may be as much as a pint."

In considering what these men and women say, note that there may be a tendency to overestimate the quantity of fluid, just as the total amount of menstrual blood (about four tablespoons) or semen (about one teaspoon) is sometimes perceived as much more than it actually is. The man who speaks about a half cup to a cup is probably exaggerating the quantity, even though his observation about the variation in amount may be correct. In the cases of female ejaculation observed by Whipple, Perry, and their colleagues, only a few drops to about a quarter of a teaspoon were usually expelled.

What is this fluid that some women expel at the moment of

orgasm? It is not the color of urine, it does not smell or taste like urine, nor does it stain like urine. The fluid has been variously described as colorless, clear, or milky, but no woman, however much she was afraid that she was urinating, has ever described the fluid as yellow in color. One woman in her mid-thirties was told by her doctor that her experiences were the result of urinary incontinence. Disbelieving him, she invented an ingenious experiment to see if this was true. After taking Urised tablets, which dye urine blue, she inspected the "wet spots" on her sheet following a number of orgasmic expulsions. No color whatsoever was apparent in some samples, and in others only the faintest bluish tinge appeared. So she intentionally released some urine on the sheet. This time the color was unmistakably a deeper blue. This enterprising woman therefore concluded that her orgasmic expulsions were not coming from the bladder.[2] One twenty-two-year-old mother of twins said that hers dried into a whitish powder and left no stain.

Women and men consistently report that the ejaculate has no odor, or certainly not the odor of urine. One woman said, "Although my doctor said it was urine, I have tasted and smelled it and know it is not." Others report that it has a taste and even a taste that varies from time to time.

A man from Oregon, the father of two and married for twenty years, wrote, "I always knew the fluid was not urine. Sometimes it is bitter but usually it is sweet. This may be caused by the woman's diet or metabolism." It has been reported that a man's ejaculatory fluid changes taste depending upon what he has eaten. That is probably also the case with the fluid expelled by women.

One woman, married for nineteen years, with children ages ten and twelve, who describes herself as a devout Christian, reported that ". . . the flavor changes four times during the month. Tangy, sour, tart, and very, very sweet. The sweet taste lasts about three days and is right before my period. It is absolutely delicious. This sweet taste is better than any honey and not nearly as thick."

Not only does the taste and appearance vary, so does its frequency. Some women have reported that they ejaculate every time they make love, others only occasionally, though some women have detected a cyclical pattern, possibly related to the phases of the menstrual cycle: "I've experienced this ejaculation with nearly every sexual experience in my thirteen years of marriage, often several times during a single lovemaking episode." "Accompanying orgasm, I experience ejaculation most of the time," said a fifty-eight-year-old grandmother. "I ejaculate about 50 percent of the time," wrote a twenty-seven-year-old registered nurse.

A twenty-six-year-old childbirth educator who describes herself as the "obese, happily married mother of two children" reports that "it happens about every sixth time we make love. The fluid is odorless and colorless, and immediately after the fluid escapes I feel a tremendous relief."

How do other men and women feel about female ejaculation? Attitudes vary from disgust to ecstasy, from puzzlement to acceptance. We were surprised by the number of people in their sixties, seventies, and eighties who reported their experiences of female ejaculation. Typical is this woman, who describes herself as "sixty-eight years young and married for the past nine years to a man six years my senior, following sixteen years of celibate life." She adds, "Thank you for answering many unspoken questions in my mind and dismissing many doubts that I was not a 'normal' woman."

And this, from a sixty-two-year-old woman, married for thirty-eight years:

*Over the years, I have very often experienced ejac-
ulation. It has been a virtual geyser of fluid, enough
to wet the bed, different from lubrication, with a
distinctive odor. Usually it occurs when I am on top.
Rather than disturbing me, my husband and I have
always related this phenomenon to heightened pleasure. Very often it was accompanied by multiple
orgasms on both our parts. I always assumed,
naively, that other women had the same experience.*

A woman of thirty-seven, with a husband of forty-three,
both "high school graduates with above-average academic and
athletic records," wrote, "I've never revealed my 'secret' simply because every article I've ever read has insisted that such a
happening is impossible. I have felt like a freak or a nympho
for many many years, and I'm sure my husband thinks so too."

A twenty-six-year-old registered nurse who is studying for
her master's degree wrote:

*The first time I ejaculated I couldn't believe it. I
have never had any trouble with stress incontinence
and had always emptied my bladder prior to a sexual encounter. In any event, it didn't seem to bother
my partner and it didn't bother me. The pleasure
overrode any negative thought.*

A twenty-eight-year-old reports that ejaculation ". . . can
have drawbacks. As I am in the upright position (which is best)
the warm liquid flowing down on my husband's genitals makes
it very hard for him to hold back."

At the other extreme, a twenty-one-year-old divorcée wrote
that her husband had become convinced that she was deliberately urinating on him every time they made love, which made

him so angry that finally one day, "He deliberately peed on me, left, and sued me for divorce."

How has it happened that a phenomenon as widely experienced as female ejaculation has not been recognized by the medical profession, and has been dismissed as Victorian pornographic fantasy, or as urinary stress incontinence? Many women report that they sought medical help to understand what was happening to them.

From Alabama a recently widowed woman reported:

> *I happen to be one of those women who for years have been asking doctors, even female doctors, for some explanation of what is going on with my body. Some said it was a weak bladder. Others just simply said that some women have more lubrication than others.*

A woman of forty-two commented:

> *After my hysterectomy, I began to experience the leaking of fluids. I was very embarrassed, and it turned me right off. Thank God I have an understanding husband. When I went to my doctor for a checkup, I told him what happened. He told me if it happens again, I will have to see a surgeon.*

And a woman of sixty, who did not follow the advice she was given, expressed relief: "After twenty years of visiting countless doctors and spending many hundreds of dollars—ten doctors told me I needed an operation for this condition—now I finally know what my 'problem' is and that I am not going crazy."

Not all physicians we heard about were indifferent or alarmist. Some were supportive but not very informative. This woman of thirty-eight, married, with three children, reported, "I asked my doctor about it and his answer was that doctors don't understand or even know where this fluid comes from— but don't be concerned, just enjoy it! I *do* enjoy it, but I also want to understand it."

Some physicians were both supportive and informative. Since 1958, urologist Bernard Hymel, M.D., has been refusing to operate on women who were referred to him for treatment of urinary stress incontinence but who were, in his professional judgment, experiencing orgasmic expulsions of fluid. He had read Gräfenberg's original work and was aware of the G spot as well as female ejaculation. He formally presented his views to his colleagues three times, and most of them thought he was crazy. He felt correct but very isolated until he met Whipple and received confirmation of his courageous stand.

A review of the historical literature on female ejaculation may shed some light on what has been known, and why it has been ignored or kept underground by laymen and professionals alike. The same cast of historical characters who described the G spot also discussed female ejaculation, and were almost totally ignored in both cases. We mentioned Aristotle, Galen, and de Graaf at the beginning of the chapter. But they were by no means the only ones who wrote about it. A notable non-scientific treatment of the subject may be found in *The Pearl*, a compilation of Victorian short novels, poems, letters, and ballads, which is replete with tales of female ejaculation, but these were dismissed as male pornographic fantasy. In 1926, Theodore H. van de Velde, M.D., published a popular marriage manual that mentioned that some women expel a liquid during orgasm.[3] Anthropologists have reported that female ejaculation actually plays an important role in the puberty rites of a certain African tribe. The Batoro of Uganda have a custom called *kachapati*, which means "spray the wall." Before a young

Batoro woman can be considered eligible for marriage, the older women of her village teach her how to ejaculate.[4]

In 1950, Gräfenberg gave a rather full description of female ejaculation in relation to pleasure. Commenting on the "occasional production of fluid at the moment of orgasm," he wrote:

> This convulsory expulsion of fluids occurs always at the acme of the orgasm and simultaneously with it. If there is the opportunity to observe the orgasm of such women, one can see that large quantities of a clear, transparent fluid are expelled not from the vulva, but out of the urethra in gushes. . . . The profuse secretions coming out with the orgasm have no lubricating significance, otherwise they would be produced at the beginning of intercourse and not at the peak of orgasm.[5]

Although Gräfenberg indicated that he had examined the fluid, he did not specify the procedures he used.

> At first I thought that the bladder sphincter had become defective by the intensity of the orgasm. Involuntary expulsion of urine is reported in sex literature. In the cases observed by us, the fluid was examined and it had no urinary character. I am inclined to believe that "urine" reported to be expelled during female orgasm is not urine, but only secretions of the intraurethral glands correlated with the erotogenic zone along the urethra in the anterior vaginal wall.[6]

Since the fluid comes out of the urethra, which is the opening through which both men and women urinate, it is important to demonstrate scientifically that female ejaculate is indeed different from urine. It has already been firmly established that the fluids expelled from the male urethra in association with orgasm are different from urine, but no one, other than Gräfenberg, had reported examining the fluids of the female, until 1980.

In that year, a research team that included Edwin Belzer, Jr., Whipple, and Perry analyzed samples of urine and ejaculate from volunteers who were instructed to abstain from contact with male seminal fluid for at least forty-eight hours before collecting their urine and ejaculation samples. The fluids were collected in the privacy of the women's homes. Then the specimens were immediately frozen and shipped to Belzer at Dalhousie University in Halifax, Nova Scotia. Results of the analysis of the fluids collected from one volunteer were reported in the *Journal of Sex Research* in February 1981.[7]

The fluids of the other subjects were also analyzed and the results were similar to those reported in this article. Chemical analysis differentiated the ejaculatory fluids from urine on the basis of four chemical tests. Two substances, tartrate-inhibited acid phosphatase, thought to be prostatic, and glucose (sugar), were substantially higher in the ejaculatory fluid than in the urine samples. Urea and creatinine (both end products of protein metabolism normally found in urine) were substantially lower in the ejaculatory than in the urine specimens.

Frank Addiego, M.D., and Whipple also sent unidentified specimens of vasectomized male ejaculatory fluids, female ejaculatory fluids, and urine specimens to local laboratories for chemical analysis. Again, tartrate-inhibited acid phosphate levels were higher in the female ejaculatory fluids than in the urine samples, although nowhere near as high as in the male fluids.

Prior to the Belzer analysis, Sevely and Bennett had done an excellent search of the literature concerning this phenomenon and published their conclusions in an article entitled "Concerning Female Ejaculation and the Female Prostate" in the *Journal of Sex Research* in February 1978. They concluded that women can ejaculate and that the fluid expelled by women through the urethra has prostatic fluid as a component. Although they did not do chemical analyses of it, their extensive review of medical and popular books led them to conclude that female sexual fluids (like male fluids) can contribute to erotic pleasure.[8]

Initially, the early genital system is the same in all human embryos. About the sixth week after conception, the differentiation begins with the gonads, then the internal genitals, and, finally, the external genitals. The ovary and testes have their common beginning in a structure that can differentiate in either direction, male or female. Embryologists and anatomists use the terms "vestigial" or "atrophied" to describe the many homologues in the adult male and female that have no apparent function and appear to be no more than the embryological vestiges of the corresponding glands or organs in the opposite sex. Every gland and organ in the male has its counterpart in the female, and vice versa.[9]

Despite all the descriptions of female ejaculation in both medical and popular literature throughout history, contemporary sexologists dismissed the phenomenon until the publication of Sevely and Bennett's article.

In 1966, Masters and Johnson wrote that female ejaculation is an "erroneous but widespread concept."[10] Kinsey, writing a few years earlier, gave the subject a bit more attention:

> Since the prostate gland and seminal vesicles are only vestigial structures in the female, she does not actually ejaculate. Muscular contractions of the

vagina following orgasm may squeeze out some of the genital secretions, and in a few cases eject them with some force. This is frequently referred to, particularly in deliberately erotic literature, as an ejaculation in the female; but the term cannot be strictly used in that connection.[11]

In *The Female Eunuch,* published in 1970, Germaine Greer stated that "all kinds of false ideas are still in circulation about women, although they were disproved years ago; many men refused to relinquish the notion of female ejaculation, which although it has a long and prestigious history, is utterly fanciful."[12]

Sevely and Bennett suggest that one reason for the lack of acceptance of female ejaculation may be a problem of language. In ancient times, the word "semen" was used to describe the "seed" or "ejaculate" of either sex. You may recall that de Graaf refers to his predecessors' supposition that this ejaculate contained "female semen," but when the microscope revealed that only the male ejaculate contained sperm, "the word previously used to describe the fluids of both sexes was allocated in the scientific literature to males alone. Since the female ejaculatory fluid did not contain 'seed,' these fluids were left without a word to describe them."[13]

The Trobriand Islanders of the South Pacific, in addition to being aware of the G spot and the importance of pelvic motion, also knew about female ejaculation. They used the same word, *momona,* for both the male and female discharge. (*Ipipisi momona* literally means "it squirts out the discharge.") The Trobrianders believe this discharge lubricates and increases pleasure. Western anthropologists, no doubt thinking that female ejaculation was a myth, have suggested that women from various Melanesian groups urinated during orgasm. But it seems highly unlikely that the Trobrianders would mistake ejaculation for urination and then describe its purpose as lubrication and pleasure.[14] Physiologically it is next to impossible for a man to urinate at the moment of orgasm, and unless a woman has a defective bladder or weak muscles, it may be equally difficult for her to do so. To suggest that the orgasms of the Trobrianders are usually accompanied by urination in the female not only contradicts the report of the islanders themselves, it is also physiologically doubtful.

Perry and Whipple took Sevely and Bennett's theories a bit further. "Without a name, female ejaculation quickly vanished from the science texts. And, deprived of its reproductive function, female ejaculate can only serve one purpose: pleasure. But the notion of women enjoying sex for its own sake is a relatively new one, and so there was little incentive to describe a fluid with no reproductive purpose."[15]

Sometimes it is not clear whether a woman is ejaculating or whether she is suffering from urinary stress incontinence. The latter can occur as a result of sneezing, coughing, laughing, jumping, or during orgasm. It may be that both can occur at the same time, although urinary incontinence is more likely to occur in women with weak pubococcygeus muscles, while female ejaculation occurs mostly in women with strong pubococcygeus muscles.

Even if urinary stress incontinence is diagnosed, it is extremely important that a complete evaluation of the pelvic muscles be done before surgery takes place. Stress incontinence can often be corrected solely through muscle training. (This is discussed in depth in chapter 4, which describes the importance of muscle tone in sexual response.)

There is apparently some risk that the ejaculatory reaction

may be diminished or eliminated as a result of surgery. Yet some women, like this thirty-six-year-old mother of three who had a hysterectomy at twenty-seven, report that surgery facilitated ejaculation:

> After my surgery, I thought I had to urinate when having sex, but it felt so good I didn't want to stop. And we knew it wasn't urine, because I've always emptied my bladder prior to intercourse. Each time I ejaculate from two to four times. I actually thought deep down inside that I was blessed to feel so good and enjoy sex. I'm not suggesting that women have hysterectomies to enjoy sex, but they should know that the womb is not necessarily (if at all) their only means of sexual gratification.

Whipple and Perry have hypothesized that women who ejaculate may be less prone to cystitis (bladder infections). This theory is supported, at least indirectly, by the remarks of one woman who apparently withheld her ejaculation: "I often have bladder infections and get severe stomach cramps after intercourse. I was wondering if it was from my trying to retain that fluid secretion during intercourse because I didn't know what it was."

Another woman put it this way:

> I am a little confused by the sensation of needing to urinate which then proceeds to pleasure. The confusion comes from the association of "the needing to void" discomfort and the onset of cystitis symptoms. Could manipulation of the G spot be connected with these symptoms? Or maybe tension results sometimes from not having "ejaculated"?

Perhaps it is only women who feel the urge to ejaculate and suppress it who may be more prone to cystitis. Further study is needed to test this, but it does seem possible that if the fluid is held back, a woman may become more easily susceptible to infection. This may be similar to the experience some women have when their breasts are filled with milk, the baby is not available to suckle, and the engorgement may also lead to infection in this gland.

Some women may experience retrograde ejaculation if the fluid shoots into the bladder rather than out of the urethra at the moment of orgasm. Perry and Whipple formulated this hypothesis because a number of women reported needing to urinate immediately after orgasm brought about by vaginal stimulation. When they did so, however, only a small amount of clear or whitish fluid that did not look like urine was released.

One woman who suffered a spinal cord injury many years ago gave this account of her experience:

> *I am a paraplegic due to a spinal-cord tumor [diagnosed] at age ten. I have been married for thir-teen years, and we have two girls. In 1962, due to constant bladder problems, my doctor performed an ileostomy [use of a segment of the small intestine for diverting urinary flow from the urethra] on me. They didn't remove the bladder. The problem was supposed to lie dormant. Well, it hasn't. Now my doctor says that I have to have my bladder removed. I am afraid, because if they don't know where the fluid is coming from, then how do they know this will solve the problem? If women ejaculate some-thing similar to seminal fluid from their own bodies through the urethra, is it possible that I am ejacu-*

lating this fluid and it is backing up and collecting in my bladder?

A counselor and sex educator reported an experience she had had a few days before giving birth and added that she knew of other women to whom this has also occurred. Shortly before her due date, she expelled a large amount of fluid, and her physician concluded that her membranes had ruptured. However, upon examining her, he discovered that the membranes were intact. The same phenomenon occurred twice more. Her husband, an M.D., took a sample of this fluid and examined it under a microscope. He concluded that it was neither urine nor amniotic fluid, although he did not know what it was. It is possible that the position or movement of the fetus had put pressure on the G spot, inducing ejaculation.

Another topic that merits study is the relationship between hormones and female ejaculation. Since we do not know specifically what tissues make up the G spot or where the ejaculatory fluid is coming from, it is difficult to speculate about hormonal influences. The size of the G spot seems to be smaller in postmenopausal women, so there may be a hormonal factor involved. In addition, we have no reports of female ejaculation in prepubescent girls. This is not surprising, since most young girls do not discuss their sexual experiences. If it is true, though, that women, like men, do not ejaculate until puberty, possibly there is also a similar hormonal effect on fluid production.

A woman who is taking supplemental hormones wrote as follows:

I am sixty. After menopause—over twenty years ago—I was put on estrogen for hot flashes. I have been on all strengths—and on none—in the inter-

*vening years. It's very obvious to both my husband
and me that there is a definite correlation between
the strength of the estrogen and the amount of fluid
expelled. The higher the dosage of estrogen, the
more fluid. When the cancer scare concerning estrogen started, I decided that during the winter
months, I would put up with the hot flashes. My
doctor shrugged his shoulders but agreed. Of course
I still had the hot flashes, but I had practically none
of the fluid. I'm back on the lowest strength now
(three weeks on—one week off) and even by the end
of that "off" week, there is an obvious difference.*

A widow of sixty-seven, who describes herself as "pretty old
and homely—but I have an older homely man who doesn't
seem to think so—thus the occasional opportunity for a partner," shared this information (but didn't want us to use her
name, since her twelve grandchildren might object):

*Shortly after my husband died, I started taking
estrogen because it was suggested that it might help
what seemed to be agitated depression. It seemed to
help my extreme nervousness as well as the hopeless
lack of energy that follows the death of a husband.
Perhaps the estrogen therapy caused an increase in
fluid, because I became more aware of it during
those years—though I'm sure it was happening
before. At sixty-five years old, a few cancer cells
showed up in a pap smear. I had a complete hysterectomy, which showed no cancer cells in anything
they removed. I still have the little spurt of fluid
during intercourse, though much less in quantity. So*

*the ovaries and uterus removal did not affect this
phenomenon. My interest in sex has waned considerably—almost entirely—since the operation, but
the little "spurt" mechanism is still working. It is
quite apart from the general lubrication mechanism. This part is not working so well, as I've had
some trouble with dryness since my hysterectomy. I
hope some ex-boyfriends find out about this and
remember and change their ideas about what was
happening at the time.*

Female ejaculation is not unique to women whose sexual ori-
entation is heterosexual. Many bisexual and homosexual
women have reported experiences with the expulsion of fluid
during orgasm. Actually, our preliminary reports indicate that
there may be a higher incidence of female ejaculation in the
lesbian population than there is among heterosexual women.
Whether this is in fact true, and if so why, remains to be inves-
tigated. Perhaps, as with the G spot, it is sometimes easier to
reach the area of sensitivity with a finger than it is through
penile contact. Or, perhaps, females may be more accepting of
the fluids expelled by other females than males seem to be.

One woman wrote to us, "As a bisexual with a proclivity
towards lesbianism, I have had an ejaculatory episode with my
female partner. It occurred with manual stimulation and was
quite a pleasant surprise to both of us."

Another woman explained:

*I experience both types of orgasm. The "Gräfenberg
Spot"-induced orgasms, however, are much different, in that they are subtle, soothing, and create tre-*

*mendous amounts of liquid gushing from the
vagina. This liquid neither looks, smells, nor feels
like urine. This sensation was first felt at age sev-
enteen and I was curious about it until a gay
woman explained it to me.*

Perry, Whipple, and their colleagues have examined some
women who have reported the expulsion of fluid from the
vagina. In these women, the opening of the urethra was found
to be located in or close to the opening of the vagina. This may
account for their reporting that the fluid was felt to be expelled
from the vagina.

Some women report having "wet dreams," as men do, waking up in a puddle of fluid that does not smell or stain like
urine. A few remember having had an erotic dream or feeling,
but others have no recollection of any kind. (Remember Lisa's
story at the start of this chapter.)

Female ejaculation, like response to G spot stimulation, is
intimately related to the strength of the pubococcygeus muscle.
As an introduction to the subject, here is what one nineteen-
year-old mother of two (who had attended childbirth classes
where Kegel exercises were taught) reported:

*Prior to learning of this exercise, I had severe prob-
lems with my bladder and kidneys. I also never
experienced an ejaculatory orgasm before. After
giving birth, I started doing this exercise to tighten
my vaginal muscles. My bladder problems have
diminished altogether, and I have ejaculatory
orgasms! My husband finds this a big turn-on, and
it makes me feel great. Maybe all women could*

experience this by doing the exercise and building
up this gland and the surrounding muscles.

Although many women will not become ejaculators, perhaps all women can enhance their sexual pleasure by doing pubococcygeus muscle exercises—which is what we will discuss in the next chapter.

·4·

The Importance of Healthy
Pelvic Muscles

From a practical point of view, the role of muscle tone is extremely important, because through education or therapy all of us can do something about our own muscle tone and positively influence our sexual responses. This is, in a way, the how-to-do-it-yourself (with a bit of help, if necessary) chapter. We assume every woman has a G spot and every man has a prostate gland. The way they function depends, in part, on the state of the surrounding muscles. Most men ejaculate, as do many women, and once again, the process of ejaculation is directly affected by the condition of the muscles that are called into play.

The muscle tone of the entire body affects sexual functioning in many important ways. People whose bodies are always contracted and tense are limited in the sensations they can feel and the emotions they can express. People whose muscles are flaccid are limited in different ways, in the manner in which they can experience and express the life within them. The muscles of the stomach, hips, and thighs are especially important to sexual experience and expression. If they are too tense, it may be difficult to move the pelvis independently of the legs and torso; if they are flaccid, it may be difficult for the pelvis to move at all. The main focus of this chapter, however, is not the general musculature, but a special muscle that surrounds and supports the sexual organs and that is closely related to genital health as well as to sexual pleasure.

The technical name for this muscle is the pubococcygeus (pronounced "pew-bo-cox-uh-gee-us"), but almost no one can remember how to pronounce it, so it is customary, even in professional circles, to refer to it as the "PC group." Several muscles make up the PC group, but we will refer to the whole group collectively because, in sexual activity, they almost always act together.

The PC muscle runs from the pubic bone in the front to the coccyx (the tailbone at the end of the spine) in the rear. In animals, this muscle wags the tail. In humans, the PC muscle supports the anus and adjacent internal organs and helps to keep them from sagging. It usually lies about an inch or so beneath the surface of the skin, and may vary from a half-inch to over two inches in thickness. Most of the muscle is innervated by the pudendal nerve, which detects stimulation around the clitoris, labia, vaginal entrance, and anus, and sends signals to the brain. The pudendal nerve also transmits signals from the brain to the PC muscle, inducing the rhythmic contractions that are associated with the most common type of orgasm. Although many experts believe that only the pudendal nerve is important to the PC muscle,[1] the deeper part of the muscle, the upper third, which is located further inside and nearer to the uterus, is also served by the pelvic nerve, one of the most complex in the human body. One branch of this nerve, it is generally agreed, connects the bladder and uterus (or male prostate) with the lower spinal cord, while a second branch

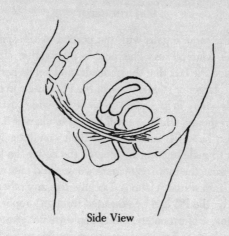

Side View

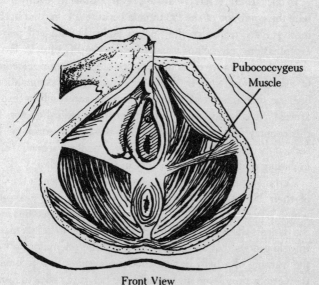

Pubococcygeus
Muscle

Front View

Illustration 4
The Pubococcygeus Muscle

connects the same organs with the portion of the spinal cord behind the solar plexus. This double innervation of the PC muscle—and the fact that the pudendal and pelvic nerves may innervate a larger or smaller area of the PC muscle in different individuals—may help explain some of the wide variations in orgasmic response, which we will discuss in chapter 5.

Men also have PC muscles, and their condition is just as important to male orgasm. In general, the better the health of the PC muscle, the more enjoyment women and men are likely to derive from sexual relations. Luckily, like any other muscle in the body, the PC can be educated through proper exercise and training. Unfortunately, most people are not aware of this.

In our culture, it has not always been possible to readily evaluate the condition of the PC muscle because it is located in the most private region of the human body. In standard pelvic examinations, physicians usually bypass the PC muscle. Even those who are aware of its importance are sometimes reluctant to ask their patients to contract it during an examination, because such intentional muscular activity can result in sexual arousal. (It is important to remember that medical doctors in this country have not been trained in the field of sexology. In fact, only in the last few years have medical schools been including material about sexuality in their curricula.)

Certain other cultures systematically train women in the use of their PC muscles. Middle Eastern dancing, for example, which is performed for the pleasure of both the spectators and the dancers themselves, also teaches the dancers to isolate many muscle groups that are usually used together. A major part of the training of a belly dancer involves learning how to isolate the various muscles in and around the pelvis in order to move them independently of each other and of the rest of the body, and even learning to use one set of stomach muscles without moving the others. Unless the PC muscle moves independently, one cannot correctly execute the belly roll, one exercise that helps prepare the dancer's body for sexual activity and for childbirth.

In the early 1940s, pioneering gynecologist Arnold Kegel, M.D., forged ahead of his colleagues by giving the PC muscle the attention it deserved. Instead of operating on women with urinary stress incontinence, he taught them how to strengthen their PC muscles through exercise. Thus, most of his patients did not have to undergo surgery and many of them experienced orgasm for the first time in their lives. Furthermore, Kegel invented a device to help him evaluate the PC muscles of his patients and to assist in training them. Called a perine-ometer, it was probably the world's first specific biofeedback device; it consisted of a small, hollow rubber cone supported on a form so that it could be inserted into the region of the vagina that is surrounded by the PC muscle. A tube connected the cone to a simple air-pressure gauge. By watching the needle on the gauge, the patient could observe the strength of the contractions of her PC muscle and, with practice, improve them.

Kegel's invention was, in many ways, a marvel of simplicity. In spite of the therapeutic advantages it afforded, its simplicity may have offended the technological bias of the twentieth century. After a brief popularity, Kegel's simple mechanical device (which cost $39.95) was gradually forgotten while some physicians experimented with new and more sophisticated operations and others used drugs to tackle the problem of uri-nary stress incontinence.

Although Kegel's perineometer was more than a step in the right direction, its main drawback was that it did not permit "absolute" readings of PC strength because its accuracy was somewhat influenced by the relative size and shape of the vagina. A small vagina would give a much higher reading than

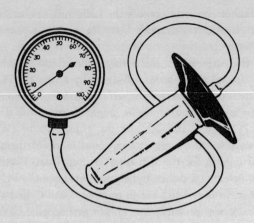

Kegel Perineometer

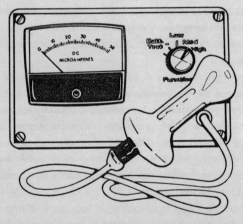

Vaginal Myograph (Electronic Perineometer)

Illustration 5

one that happened to be larger. A second drawback was that the needle in Kegel's gauge fluttered constantly in response to very slight tensing and relaxing of the PC muscle, making it necessary to "guesstimate" the average reading. Additionally, the shape of the device required that it be held in place with one hand during use, which led to further inaccuracies in the readings.

Since Kegel's time, interest in biofeedback has burgeoned, and there are now a wide variety of reliable instruments available. In 1976, Perry invented a "vaginal myograph," which can provide both visual and auditory information about muscle activity, to be used in conjunction with a conventional EMG (electro-myographic) biofeedback device.

The vaginal myograph is made of smooth plastic in the shape of a small dumbbell, which can be easily inserted into the vagina like a tampon. Once in place, it does not need to be held. Silver strip sensors on the myograph are placed so that they come into contact with the PC muscle area. Using a standard EMG machine, the vaginal myograph permits absolute readings of both the contractions *and* the resting state of the muscle. Unlike Kegel's perineometer, it can be inserted by the woman while she is fully clothed. (See Appendix A for further information about this device and other aids.)

But we are getting ahead of ourselves. Before discussing in detail how the PC muscle may be examined and trained with biofeedback equipment, let's first consider why the PC muscle may need evaluation and training, what can go wrong with it, and how women and men can find their own PC and, if necessary, learn to bring it under voluntary control.

The most common problem is simply weakness of the PC muscle, which is often accompanied by atrophy (shrinkage). In the 1940s, Kegel photographed young girls who already showed a pronounced relaxation of the pelvic area. What brings about such a condition so prematurely is only partially understood, and, although of great importance, a discussion of the causes of this problem is beyond the scope of this book. It is more common for weakness or atrophy to occur later in life, and both conditions may result in a variety of physical problems. Included are uterine prolapse, cystocele, and rectocele, which refer respectively to displacement of the uterus, bladder, or rectum into the vaginal area as a result of poor muscle tone. In addition, several functional problems may arise, the most common of which is urinary stress incontinence. It is estimated that at least 80 percent of urinary stress incontinence may be traced to the weakness of the PC muscle, which is why Kegel's exercise treatment was so successful. Recent research has also confirmed Kegel's belief that weak PC muscles may be partially responsible for failure to reach orgasm during intercourse.

It has been widely assumed that weak PC muscles are a *result* of childbirth trauma. But Kegel and others[2] observed that weak muscles were more often the *cause* of problems with childbirth, and today many experts are prescribing prenatal exercises to strengthen the PC muscle. Nevertheless, millions of young mothers will still enter the delivery room today without any training or preparation for childbirth and with weak PC muscles that contribute to difficult deliveries.

Weakness of the PC muscle is also often a factor in vaginal anesthesia (lack of sensation). A flabby, unexercised muscle is not very responsive; a healthy muscle is more sensitive to physical stimulation. Sometimes complaints about lack of enjoyment of vaginal penetration are rooted not so much in psychological problems, but in lack of physical fitness, although one can never totally separate the psychological from the physical, and the flabbiness of the muscle may, in fact, have a psychological basis.

It is well known that if any muscle is not properly exercised, it may become weak and atrophied. For example, if your broken arm has been in a cast, it will take some time, effort, and exercise to restore the muscles to their former size and strength after the cast is removed. Yet people imagine that the sexual muscles can remain inactive for long periods of time and then miraculously resume full functioning as soon as the right partner comes along. Unfortunately, the PC muscle may also take time to recover from disuse.

> *Ruth was a nurse-midwife in her late twenties who had always enjoyed sexual relations and also trained her patients to practice Kegel exercises. At a conference, she learned about the vaginal myograph and was eager to use it and satisfy her curiosity about her own PC muscle. Ruth claimed to be multiply orgasmic but she registered only 9 microvolts, a relatively low score. From her sexual history we would have predicted that her reading would be twice as high. When questioned, Ruth revealed that during the preceding year she had not been sexually active and now, with her present partner, whom she was planning to marry, she could not achieve orgasm. She had attributed her anorgasmia to "communication problems" that she despaired of resolving.*
>
> *Like many responsive women, Ruth had kept her PC muscle in good shape by masturbating in her youth and, as a young adult, by having frequent intercourse. During the year of abstinence from sexual activity, it never occurred to her to do Kegel exercises, because she associated them only with preparation for childbirth. But some weeks after*

being given a twenty-minute crash course in bio-feedback-assisted Kegel exercises, she wrote a letter confirming that strengthening her PC muscles had successfully resolved her "communications problem."

Kegel exercises involve sustained and short contractions of the PC muscle alternating with equal periods of relaxation. Before describing them in detail, let's consider other types of problems related to the condition of the PC.

Less well known but almost as common a problem is pelvic tension. Tension in the PC muscle, like tension in other muscles, may be situational (triggered by a particular event) or chronic. The most common form of situational tension is vaginismus, in which the PC muscle clamps down so tightly at the approach of the penis (even the penis of a trusted partner) that penetration becomes difficult, painful, or even impossible. Although vaginismus is usually emotional in origin, the standard treatment for it is often physical. Using progressively larger dilators to gradually force the vagina to accept larger and larger intrusions may help women to discover that the vaginal opening is expandable. However, we believe that biofeedback is a gentler, more effective method.

Michelle was a frail woman who had had a very difficult delivery with her second child. Her physician had warned her that another pregnancy might result in her death. Her medical history precluded the use of birth control pills or an IUD (intrauterine device), and unfortunately her husband abhorred the diaphragm, condoms, and vaginal spermicides. The psychological origin of her vaginismus was obvious—penile penetration might be fatal. After

> *some discussion, she agreed to be fitted for a cervical cap, which resolved the contraception problem but not the vaginismus. Biofeedback training was therefore recommended. After becoming familiar with the device, she was able to insert the vaginal myograph by herself without difficulty. After less than one hour of training in muscle relaxation, she began to evidence good control over her balking PC muscle. A week later she reported that vaginismus was no longer a problem.*

Michelle's difficulty surfaced in a sexual context, but many other problems are probably associated with chronic pelvic tension. Most people are aware that when any muscle remains tense for an extended period of time, it begins to ache. When this continues, awareness of the pain may fade because sensation depends on movement, and until the tension either increases or decreases, no movement occurs. Some clinicians believe that often what is described as "lower-back pain" is really PC muscle tension. It does seem more acceptable to say that one's back hurts than to admit to vaginal tension. Often lack of awareness makes accurate perception difficult. We have treated a number of patients who initially complained of lower-back pain and found relief by learning to relax their PC muscles.

Chronic PC muscle tension may masquerade as pain in other parts of the body as well:

> *Mary is a forty-year-old psychotherapist who has suffered from a "slightly" ulcerated colon for several years. By "slightly," her physician meant that he could find no physical evidence of damage, but it was the best explanation he could come up with for*

her abdominal cramping. When Mary finally tried biofeedback therapy, she reported that she had difficulty finding acceptable sexual outlets, although she often got "turned on" during the course of her working day. She never masturbated, one way to relieve this sort of tension. When she finally decided to try masturbating, rather than putting up with unacceptable partners or continuing with chronic tension, she reported that her "slightly ulcerated colon" vanished permanently.

(Of course, this may have been an irritable bowel syndrome associated with stress, which in no way detracts from the conclusion drawn.)

Early and still very preliminary research by Perry suggests that chronic pelvic tension may be responsible for or contribute to certain other common medical problems. Women who have been tested and have high resting levels of PC tension report that they suffer from frequent vaginal and urinary tract infections, such as cystitis and monilia.

Francine loved sex and described herself as "always horny." She was also devoutly religious and devoted to her husband, who enjoyed sex as much as she did. He thought it was the best way to begin and end every day. During their first year of marriage, everything was perfect except that Francine suffered from recurrent bouts of cystitis. Over a ten-month period, she consulted her doctor eight times. The only explanation he could offer was that sometimes newlyweds have "too much sex," which can cause what is often referred to as "honeymoon cys-

titis." Francine didn't think twice a day was excessive, so she continued to take antibiotics month after month.

A routine examination with a vaginal myograph revealed that Francine had a highly developed PC muscle. In fact, she was in the top percentile in terms of contractile strength. But it also revealed that she was unable to relax her PC muscle. Francine's "relaxed" level was actually higher than the "maximum contraction" level of the average woman tested. Her personal history quickly revealed the reason for her chronic pelvic tension. Her father was a very suspicious and authoritarian man who believed that "all public toilets are full of germs." From kindergarten on, Francine was taught that no matter how badly she might have to urinate, she should hold it in until she got home. So she learned to tighten her PC muscle and could go for hours, long past the point where the rest of us might have wet our pants.

Whether or not chronic pelvic tension contributes to vaginal and urinary tract infections has not yet been determined; however, it is clear that a muscle that is constantly taut contributes to poor circulation of blood and lymph. (Make a fist, and notice your knuckles turn white as the blood is squeezed out of the tissue. That's what happens to a PC muscle, too, under constant tension.) When circulation is impaired, it is difficult for the white blood cells to do their natural job of searching out and destroying germs. Too frequently, antibiotics are prescribed without considering the possibility of functional causes and cures—like learning to relax a tense muscle so that the body can prevent illness or help to heal itself. It is also difficult to estimate how many women have been offended by the implication that their recurrent infections are due to "promiscuity." (The presence of certain microorganisms in the vagina does not in itself produce infection. It is, rather, the physiological condition of the vagina and urinary tract that determines which microorganisms will thrive.)[3]

Undiagnosed chronic pelvic tension may also contribute to more severe problems. Another of our early research subjects registered extremely high pelvic tension, some 35 to 40 microvolts lasting for several minutes. Although she was invited to take advantage of free therapy for her condition, she was unable to do so because of a new job in a distant city. Several months later Perry learned that she had developed cervical cancer and hypothesized that the chronically impaired circulation, especially in and around the cervix, may have made her more susceptible to the disease.

Besides weakness or excessive tension, there is another condition peculiar to the PC muscle: lack of control. As mentioned earlier, we frequently encounter patients who express complete ignorance of their ability to contract or relax this muscle. Many don't even know where it is. We have observed intense muscular contractions of the PC muscle, comparable in intensity to a "charley horse" or cramp in the leg muscle, while the patient seemed totally unaware of the dramatic muscular events taking place in and around her vagina. Menstrual cramps may be related to exactly this type of tension.

In most areas of the human body, a muscle that contracted unpredictably, or alternately contracted and relaxed in such a fashion, would quickly receive professional attention. Why is the opposite often true with respect to the PC muscle? Many people, and especially women, have been trained *not* to pay attention to sensations in the pelvic region. In the process of overlooking sexual arousal, many people learn to disregard the signals that would enable them to control their PC muscle.

One way people avoid pelvic sensation is by chronically tensing those muscles. Commenting on a therapy session she had led, one bioenergetic analyst reported:

> *The majority of women couldn't move and weren't aware that they couldn't because they were so tense in their pelvic area. When I would have them start to move their pelvises, they would find out how much it actually hurt to do it and how guilty they felt when they did. They would bring up the whole issue of what they were told about their bodies and sex. Besides teaching them to move their pelvises, I also taught them how to let their tummies hang out. I would have them stand the way they usually do, like they were taught to, and then stand the other way so they could feel the difference and find out how rigid they were and how much they were holding in that area. I began to get reports that their sex lives were improving, that they were having more frequent orgasms, and that they were more relaxed, particularly in man/woman situations.*

(There is, of course, good reason for being able to contract *and* relax the abdominal muscles, since as with the PC muscle both abilities are important.)

The rise in popularity of the tampon may also, inadvertently, have contributed to lack of awareness of PC muscle activity. As the tampon swells, stimulating the PC muscle, some women may begin to experience sensations they would rather ignore. The more often this occurs, the less awareness these women may have of other sensations in the vaginal area.

Sometimes an individual's medical history reveals an even more extreme example of this cultivated nonawareness. Linda, thirty-one, was referred for therapy because she complained of a total absence of feeling in and around her genitals.

When she was in her mid-twenties, Linda had checked into the local hospital for what she thought was the removal of a small growth on her cervix. When she awoke from the anesthesia, she was informed that a total hysterectomy had been performed. She said that she had received no counseling (except that she was advised to avoid sex until at least two weeks after the pain went away). In later discussions, it became clear that her physician had not anticipated the intense emotional and physical pain that she had experienced after the unexpected loss of her reproductive organs. She had reacted to this "pain" by learning to disregard it. When she later discovered that she could not experience any sexual sensations at all, she assumed that her physician had accidentally cut her "sexual nerves" during the hysterectomy. He told her it was all in her head, and recommended that she consult a psychiatrist. The psychiatrist was more interested in her relationship with her father than she was, so she stopped seeing him. For six years she lived with the stigma of being "frigid."

Evaluation with vaginal myography revealed that her PC muscle was spasmodically contracting and relaxing without any awareness on her part. Routine tests of ten-second contractile strength showed

*great variation, from a high of 25 microvolts to a
low of 5.*

*Corrective therapy was relatively simple. Linda
observed the biofeedback from her PC muscle,
which convinced her that her nerves were, in fact,
intact. She was then told how to do Kegel exercises,
and encouraged to practice with biofeedback for
about one hour. The process of learned nonawareness was explained, and she was asked to include her
husband in her daily routine of PC exercises. At a
follow-up visit a week later, she demonstrated a normal degree of muscle control, and promised to continue to practice at home. Tears came to her eyes as
she expressed joy over the realization that the trouble wasn't all in her head.*

These, then, are a few of the things that may go wrong with
the PC muscle: it may atrophy, become too weak, too tense, or
out of control. It may, of course, be in excellent condition. If
you have none of the problems described above, and are not in
the age category in which you may want to consider PC muscle
exercise as an alternative to hormone replacement therapy to
improve vaginal lubrication, you still may be interested in
doing PC muscle exercises solely to improve your enjoyment
of sex.

In the early days of sex research, it was assumed that vascular (blood flow) activity was the "primary" causal mechanism in sexual response. But research with the vaginal
myograph, and with male subjects using a smaller rectal
myograph, has shown that there is significant activity in the PC
muscle *before* there is any erectile response in the male or
lubricative response in the female. In terms of precise awareness of internal muscular activity, women are once again very

much like men—both sexes tend to overlook the minute "twitches" of the PC muscle that constitute the very first stage of sexual response.

When a woman contracts her PC muscle, blood rushes into the vaginal tissue *after* each contraction, making the tissue darker and increasing lubrication. Sex therapists often counsel women who lubricate slowly to stall their partners until they are "really ready." In view of our present knowledge, it would be more helpful to suggest an active strategy, advising women to exercise their PC muscle, thereby speeding up the process of lubrication. This knowledge is especially useful for those older women who may suffer from dryness of the vaginal lining. Estrogen cream is one method that has been used to help with this problem, but some physicians believe that there is a risk of cancer involved in its use. PC muscle exercises may accomplish the same goal, without the risk of cancer.

For years, physicians inadvertently took responsibility for the PC muscle away from its owners. They used three methods to do this—surgical, chemical, and electrical, the first by far the most common. Close to fifty varieties of surgical procedures have been applied to the PC muscle and surrounding areas to control urinary stress incontinence.[4]

During the middle third of the twentieth century most surgical attempts were rather crude. In essence, the PC muscle was cut and retied, in the hope that a lump of scar tissue would form and provide more clamping power on the urinary passage. In time, further sagging of the PC required another cut and, hopefully, another lump. Yet a few gynecologists always insisted that exercise be tried before surgery.[5] No research adequately considered the effect of such surgery on sexual response, so little is known about the possibly harmful side-effects of this approach.

In recent years, surgical procedures have grown more sophisticated. Now the length, angle, size, and shape of the urethra are first carefully studied with X rays and ultrasound, but the basic method is still the same: rearrangement of the urethra or muscle tissues with little or no attempt to involve the patient in helping herself.

Many physicians have criticized the willingness of some surgeons to rush in with the knife, and recommend chemical intervention as a first step. Drugs are used to block the muscular activity that might cause leakage. Again, usually no attempt is made to deal with the essential inactivity of the muscle system that may have created the problem in the first place.

After the Second World War, electrical therapy was introduced and has been advocated from time to time since then. Electrodes—similar to those in certain slenderizing machines that were in vogue during the 1950s—were used to induce muscular activity. Some researchers shocked their subjects with short bursts of high-voltage electricity, while others attempted to isolate the appropriate natural frequencies of the region (something like what a pacemaker does for the heart muscles). In either case, the woman would passively receive a course of treatment that did little to cure the incontinence.

More recently, a variety of inexpensive devices have been patented that insert the electrodes directly into the vagina. They are battery-operated and are supposed to be safe for use at home. We experimented briefly with these devices, combining them with biofeedback (non-shock) therapy, but women found them so distasteful (several categorically refused to continue with them) that we now only use them in rare instances. One woman editor described them as "miniature cattle prods."

A few published studies have claimed to demonstrate the effectiveness of these electrostimulation devices, but they all contain serious methodological flaws. In every study we have seen, the electrical treatment is combined with the use of Kegel exercises, and it is not possible to ascertain whether the beneficial results come from the electrostimulation plus exercise or the exercise alone. Since no evidence is presented to demonstrate that electrostimulation adds anything to the exercise, exercise by itself seems to us the more likely cause. It is also cheaper, safer, and more pleasant.

If you would like to learn more about the condition of your PC muscle, the first step is to consider your personal history. Have you ever leaked a small amount of urine under stress— for example, when laughing, playing sports, running, jumping? If so, you may have some PC muscle weakness or atrophy. Have you ever had difficulty reaching orgasm? That may be another indication of muscle weakness.

If you are bothered by lower-back pain, frequent vaginal or urinary infections, pain on vaginal penetration, or lack of vaginal sensitivity, the problem may be chronic pelvic tension. If you suffer from severe menstrual cramps, or wide variations in your sexual response, consider the possibility of muscle control problems.

A partner's perceptions of you may be another useful source of information. If you have a partner who can tell when you intentionally contract your PC during intercourse, you can probably rule out control problems. If your partner remarks about how snug you feel, you can probably rule out PC weakness. If your partner indicates by word or gesture that he or she cannot feel much contact, then you may suspect weak PC muscles.

Rebecca and her husband came to a clinic for help because he complained that her vagina had become so loose that he could no longer tell when his penis had slipped out. Even if he was exaggerating, the problem was real. After two weeks of biofeedback training, he remarked that she had "gone from being like an open window to being like a keyhole!" At first the therapist assumed that "some men are never happy," but after she had measured Rebecca's PC muscle with the vaginal myograph, the importance of teaching how to contract and how to relax the PC muscle became clear. Rebecca had only learned to tighten her PC muscle. Control and relaxation were the next step.

After considering your history, the next step is to find your PC muscle. This can be done alone or with a partner. We suggest you begin your self-examination with a small mirror. For some women, looking at their genitals will present no problem at all. But many women feel even more timid about viewing their genitals than they do about touching them. (Since men are accustomed to seeing their genitals, they are much less likely to feel this way.) If you are reluctant or afraid to look at yourself, consider that your genitals are, after all, part of *your* body and that you should not be ashamed of what nature or God has given you. It is relatively easy, of course, to write these words but a lot more difficult to act on them, especially when years of training have led some women (and men) to feel deeply ashamed about this part of their bodies.

To learn more about your own PC muscle, lie on your back and use your mirror to look at your genital area. If this is the first time you have ever seen your genitals, take a few minutes to see if you can identify the different parts—the vagina, the clitoris, the labia, the urethra, and the anus. (See Illustration 3, page 67.)

Once you are comfortable with looking at yourself, and have become familiar with what you are seeing, then begin to alternately pull up (as if you were holding in urine) and push down (as if you were having a bowel movement). Keep looking in the mirror. If you have good control and reasonably strong muscles, you should be able to see the perineum move in and out in response to your commands. While you are watching this area, notice whether your stomach, buttocks, and thigh muscles move at the same time. If they do, you have not yet learned to isolate the PC muscle.

There is a difference between what you need to do to educate your PC muscle and what you do for sexual enjoyment. In general, as far as sex is concerned, the more the muscles become involved, the better. That is why sexually active women may initially have difficulty isolating the PC muscle. But in order to exercise enough to improve its functioning, you must first learn how to move it independently of other muscles. The more you can isolate it, the more effective the exercise will be and the more exercise you can do without becoming tired.

The next step also involves the mirror. Many women are able to rotate their pelvises and spread their legs in such a way that the vaginal entrance will open slightly. If you can do this, with good lighting you may be able to observe some opening and closing of the vaginal entrance in response to contracting and relaxing the PC muscle. This, too, will give you some idea of the amount of control and muscle strength you have. If you cannot relax enough for the vaginal entrance to open, it may be an indication of chronic pelvic tension.

The third step in evaluating your PC muscle is to use your finger to explore the inside of your vagina. It is relatively easy to identify your PC muscle by inserting a finger in the vagina (or in the rectum if you are a man). When you first put your finger into your vagina, alternately contract and relax your PC muscle, as you did when looking in the mirror, to get an idea of where it is. The vaginal walls are relatively uniform, but with your fingers you should be able to detect the PC muscle beneath the surface all the way around, one or two inches in from the entrance. Bend your finger at a slight angle and press against the vaginal wall at intervals of about half an inch along a straight line from the entrance, going in towards the cervix (the entrance to the uterus). At each point, tighten your PC muscle and notice whether your finger can feel any movement.

According to Kegel, a healthy muscle may be three fingers thick, whereas a weak one may be "as narrow and thin as a pencil." If you test the vaginal wall every half inch, you should be able to feel the muscle at one, two, or even three intervals. You should also be able to recognize when you are pressing in front of the PC and you have gone past it, and to reach around and press against the back side, too. If you feel uncomfortable about touching your vagina, an electrical stimulator may be useful at first in helping you to identify the PC muscle. With practice, you may gain more confidence and overcome your aversion to touching yourself.

After using one finger, try the "two-finger test." Insert two fingers, side by side, as deeply as you can with comfort. Then spread your fingers apart like the opening of a pair of scissors. Now, by contracting your PC muscle, try to force your fingers to come together. If you can, fine. If that is difficult, read on— you need exercise.

If you are doing these exercises with a partner, you may want your partner to examine you first with one and then two fingers. Besides noticing how strong or weak the muscle feels, begin to notice whether some parts of your vagina are more responsive to touch than others.

The finger examination should not be used to compare one person's PC muscle with another's, since anatomical variations in the size of the vagina and factors like the overall amount of body fat have a great influence on one's subjective impression. And remember, there is no set relationship between the size of the vagina and the strength of the PC. One woman may have a large vagina with very good muscles, while another may have a small, tight vagina with poor muscles.

Some women are accustomed to flexing their pelvic muscles *only* in a sexual context, and may not be able to move them at all in a nonsexual or, worse yet, a clinical setting. Two years ago, when we were researching pelvic muscle strength using the vaginal myograph, some subjects were tested in a biofeedback therapist's office, where they were seated in a reclining chair, while others were tested in a women's health clinic, where they were lying on a standard gynecological examining table. One woman was tested in both places, and showed considerably weaker readings while she was lying on the table, so we went back and checked our data. Sure enough, there was a significant difference in muscle strength, depending on *where* the examination was conducted.

Another good method of identifying the PC muscle is to attempt to interrupt the flow of urine. If you have good muscles and good control, you can start and stop the flow of urine with precision. If you cannot do that the first time, don't despair. Learning to contract (or relax) the right muscle is part of the exercise.

We have talked a lot about the importance of correctly identifying the PC muscle before describing what exercises to do for a very important reason. Many women, after hearing about Kegel's exercises, have spent months and even years using the wrong set of muscles and accomplishing nothing.

> *Betsy, a nurse in her forties, had been doing what she believed to be Kegel exercises for over ten years. She became convinced that something serious was wrong with her bladder, because, in spite of diligent practice, stress incontinence was getting progressively worse. Finally she consulted a biofeedback specialist. Initial testing with the vaginal myograph showed that she had very weak muscles. An evaluation of her method of doing Kegel exercises revealed that she had been using primarily her buttocks and abdominal muscles instead of her PC. Practice with biofeedback brought steady improvement in muscle strength and ended the stress incontinence. Even more important to Betsy, after a few months of regular exercise, she became orgasmic with vaginal stimulation alone, something she had always hoped for but never achieved.*

Betsy's story is especially important because it illustrates that even health professionals who have studied anatomy can exercise the wrong muscles without being aware of it, and may be as deficient in body awareness as other people.

Once you have correctly identified the PC muscle, either through the finger test or the urine-flow exercise, the next step is to begin regular exercise.

There are two ways to exercise your PC muscle, with and without a resistive device in the vagina. There are substantial advantages, though, to having something against which to contract and relax the muscle. When Kegel advised his patients to exercise, he instructed them to do so while using his perineometer. Exercise without a resistive device is useful for keeping the PC muscle flexed and the vagina moist, but will not correct an atrophied muscle that needs to increase in size as well as strength.

Apparently Kegel never provided his patients with any kind of written handout or exercise manual, and though his clinical writings describe the exercises he suggested for his patients, these descriptions are slightly different in each case. Thus, one may encounter a wide assortment of divergent instructions, both from clinicians and in books. It is possible that one reason many physicians become convinced that exercise is not really an effective means of correcting the physical problem may be that without a set of detailed, consistent guidelines they themselves are unable to give their patients adequate instructions on how the exercises should actually be performed. For example, they often neglect to recommend the use of a resistive device.

What kind of a device is recommended and where can one get it? The resistive device need not be expensive. Your finger is an acceptable substitute. Apart from that, there are various devices ranging from dildos and vibrators, to new products with a nonsexual shape and color that can be purchased by mail if you are reluctant to buy one in person. (See Appendix A for details.) Whatever device you choose, it should be moderately firm but with some give. Some women have reported that hard plastic devices, such as penis-shaped vibrators, have been irritating.

Let's talk about practice with resistance first. Since improvement in PC muscle function requires frequent, regular practice, set aside at least two fifteen-minute periods a day. Pick a time when you are not likely to be interrupted. Lock the door, take the phone off the hook, and, if necessary, post a Do Not Disturb sign.

Using your resistive device, squeeze the PC muscle for three seconds and then relax it for the same amount of time. Do this ten times in a row. If it is difficult to hold the contraction for three seconds at first, hold it for two or even one second. As you build up strength and endurance, gradually increase the interval until you have worked up to ten seconds. Do not skip the equal period of relaxation. That is as important as the contraction. After you have done a series of ten contractions and relaxations, practice short flicks with your PC muscle. Squeeze and release the muscle as quickly as possible for several minutes. At first you may find it difficult to tell whether you are contracting or relaxing, but gradually it will become easier. One musically inclined woman told us that it was like learning to play a trill on the piano. She used to put on her favorite music and practice moving her PC muscle in time to it. As she became more adept, she tapped out tunes with her PC and asked her husband to guess what she was playing.

How many contractions should you do during one exercise session? Kegel often said that three hundred contractions *per day* were necessary for noticeable improvement (he was talking about contractions monitored by his perineometer and held for several seconds each). That many contractions may be excessive, especially during the first weeks. Like any other exercise program, it is prudent to start out gradually in order to avoid aching muscles. But three hundred contractions per day, approximately one hundred at a time, is probably a reasonable goal for therapeutic purposes. As you progress, sustained practice over time is more important than doing so many contractions at once, which can get boring and cause people to stop practicing prematurely.

Exercise without a resistive object has the big advantage that it can be done anywhere, anytime, and without anyone knowing what you are doing. The same exercises just described can be done without a resistive device while driving a car, eating dinner, listening to a lecture, playing bridge, or typing a manuscript. We call this spontaneous practice. Our research has shown that people who say they enjoy sex and engage in it with some regularity also frequently activate their PC muscle during the course of the day.

You can encourage yourself by placing some kind of a reminder where you will see it. For example, affix a brightly colored dot to your briefcase, the telephone, the refrigerator, a clock, or a lamp. Every time you see the dot, contract your PC muscle several times. Another approach is to utilize a frequently occurring event. One traveling saleswoman has gotten into the habit of contracting her PC muscle every time she stops at a traffic light. A stockbroker does several quick contractions when the telephone rings. Find some regularly occurring event, and practice every time it happens.

While you are practicing either fixed or spontaneous exercises, begin to notice your responses. Many people unconsciously flex their PC muscles whenever they have sexually exciting thoughts. This may lead to vaginal lubrication. Some women who become lubricated when they see someone they are sexually attracted to may be flexing their PCs without being aware of it. If your muscles are weak, or if you are out of touch with them, you may have failed to develop this habit.

After you have been exercising regularly for several weeks, you may want to redo the finger test or the urine-flow exercise to see if you notice any difference from the first time you did it. Feedback about your progress is important because even small changes in the right direction can provide encouragement and the incentive to continue. It is easy to become discouraged and quit prematurely. With unmonitored exercise, it may take one or two months before clear signs of progress appear.

If you have access to a clinician with a device for measuring the PC muscle, that can be very helpful, and it is essential for women with problems that require PC muscle evaluation or training. Most equipment, such as the vaginal myograph, is too expensive for people to own individually, but there are distinct advantages to using it. The most important one is correct diagnosis: Is the muscle too weak, or is it chronically contracted? Equipment can also help to ensure that the proper muscle is being exercised. Finally, progress can be precisely quantified so that week-to-week changes can be compared. When a digital readout or strip-chart record is provided, even small improvements are recorded and can provide encouragement. Without effective monitoring, there is a substantially higher incidence of discouragement, failure, or slower progress.

Often your partner may notice a change in your PC muscle before you do. If you are involved in a heterosexual relationship, practice PC contractions during intercourse. Ask your partner if he can feel them. Depending on how weak your muscles are to start with, it may take a few days or perhaps even a couple of weeks, but before long he'll notice them. (If he is a good sport, you can then turn the tables. Ask him to contract his PC muscle while inside of you. This will strengthen his muscle, elevate his penis towards his belly button, and perhaps also stimulate your Gräfenberg spot. If you cannot feel his contractions, perhaps he needs to read this chapter and begin a program of regular exercise too.)

Remember that without *regular* practice, no improvement can be expected. For example:

> *Marcy was not really interested in improving her PC muscle or her sexual response, but her boyfriend insisted, so she came in three or four times within a*

period of six months. Each time she registered about 3 microvolts (very weak) when measured with the vaginal myograph. She admitted that she had not done any exercises and that she had only come at the urging of her boyfriend. (Eventually they broke up, and she never returned.)

One the other hand, diligent practice can bring about surprisingly swift changes:

Dorothy was a young mother who was preoccupied with her children and became less and less interested in sex. Her husband reacted to this by having an affair, during which he discovered the advantages of strong PC muscles. He told his wife about his affair and what he had discovered, and threatened to get a divorce if she did not get medical help for her weak muscles.

Dorothy, a deeply religious person, was upset about her husband's affair, but also recognized that she had a problem. After reading books on the subject, she visited her gynecologist and, in the course of the pelvic exam, asked his opinion about the condition of her PC muscle. To her amazement this physician said he did not know what she was talking about.

Frustrated, she tried for six months to figure out how to do the exercises herself, but with little success. Finally she learned of a biofeedback therapist who offered vaginal myography, and made an appointment. According to the therapist, "She was the best patient I ever treated. She was literally motivated by the fear of Hell and damnation. Con-

*vinced that her impending divorce was caused by
her neglect of her PC muscle and determined to
save her marriage, she practiced like mad. On initial
evaluation, her muscles registered very low but
when she returned in just one week, after doing
approximately 300 ten-second contractions a day,
she was doing better than the average American
woman. By the second week, she was hitting a reading of 19 or 20, which put her in the top 2 percent
of women who have been measured." Obviously
there were other problems in the marriage that had
to be treated with marital therapy, but her husband
never again complained about her muscle weakness.*

Earlier in this chapter we mentioned that the exercise
approach to PC muscle problems has "no harmful side-effects."
Yet there is one side-effect that does cause many problems—
exercising the PC muscle can lead to sexual arousal, and
women are seldom prepared for this. When exercise is recommended for medical reasons, such as stress incontinence, therapists often neglect to mention the possibility of heightened
sexual feelings. What should be viewed as pleasurable and a
sign of good health instead sometimes produces anxiety and
guilt.

In the course of our research, we interviewed hundreds of
women who had tried, at one time or another, to conduct their
own exercise program but quit before their problems were
resolved. In many instances where we have been able to
explore the reasons for this, we discovered that unresolved sexual arousal was an important factor.

Since it is not at all unusual for women who begin PC muscle
exercises to notice an increase in their desire for sexual relations, one "problem" with exercise-induced arousal is what to

do about it. If you have a partner who is not threatened by your increased sexual desire, there is an obvious and mutually rewarding solution. Another satisfying outlet is masturbation.

That topic is quite controversial. Many women have been trained from a very early age not to touch their genitals. Some religions teach that it is sinful for either a man or a woman to engage in what is viewed as "self-abuse." For people who are members of such a group, masturbation is obviously not the answer. But there is also a positive view of masturbation, which regards it as a natural, pleasurable activity that begins at a very early age and maintains that "excessive" preoccupation with masturbation is a result, not a cause, of other difficulties.

We believe there are important physical as well as psychological reasons for masturbating. It is the best way to learn exactly how your own body responds. It provides an opportunity for experimenting alone with ways of touching, places to touch, and ways of achieving sexual satisfaction. It frees one from the compulsion to be involved with a partner when a suitable person is not available. Sometimes one also learns things about oneself through masturbation that are useful to share with a partner. If you are afraid to share such discoveries with your partner, it may tell you something about the relationship.

Only about one-third of American women masturbate with any regularity, compared to two-thirds of American men. Generally speaking, women who masturbate regularly seem to be less susceptible to problems with muscle weakness than women who do not. Two factors may play a role here. Women who masturbate are probably in better touch with the feelings in their pelvic area. Masturbation, if it results in orgasm, also insures regular exercise of the PC muscle, which leads to greater awareness of genital sensation. The spiral can go both ways, lack of awareness leading to less frequent masturbation, to less frequent exercise of the PC muscle, and thus to weakness or atrophy.

The major part of this chapter has been devoted to the PC muscles of women because in our society more women than men seem to suffer from severe weakness of the PC muscle. Although the reasons for this are really beyond the scope of this book, some of them at least should be obvious. Nevertheless, many men do suffer from weak PC muscles. One symptom of this condition is a long refractory period, the interval during which another erection is not possible. Recent research has supplied convincing evidence that men are just as capable of multiple orgasm as women, and a strong PC muscle seems to be the most important factor contributing to that capacity.

Men can find their PC muscle by feeling inside the rectum in the same way that women palpate the muscle by feeling inside the vagina. They can do the same finger test and urine-flow exercise, and spontaneous exercise is just as beneficial for them. Perry has designed a rectal myograph, a smaller version of the vaginal myograph, for use in training men (or women with vaginismus) to gain control over their PC muscles. Sustained contractions alternating with relaxation, as well as fluttering the PC muscle rapidly, are equally useful for both men and women. Another beneficial exercise men can practice is the "towel trick." A man with a healthy PC muscle should be able to hang a small towel over his erect penis and raise and lower it at will by contracting the muscle. If a hand towel slips off, try a lighter washcloth. If the muscle is weak, start with a handkerchief. Because a firm erection is needed for the towel trick, many men will want to practice in private at first, since "performance anxiety" is the archenemy of male erection.

When we examine the historical evidence, it becomes clear that our discoveries about the importance of a healthy PC muscle are anything but new. In 1926, van de Velde published what was to become the most popular sex manual of the next quarter-century: *Ideal Marriage: Its Physiology and Technique*. Before Masters and Johnson came along, his book went through over forty printings and influenced millions of people. Nearly sixty years later, although we know more about human anatomy and physiology—the role of hormones, for example—van de Velde's aesthetic understanding of sexuality has never been surpassed.

In fact, van de Velde knew all about the sexual importance of good voluntary control of the PC muscle, and clearly stated what later researchers have rediscovered over and over again, namely, that some women are "especially adept and expert" at controlling this muscle "at will—a faculty of enormous value in the *technique* of intercourse. . . . Yet the gymnastics of the pelvic floor is totally neglected by women, almost without exception."[6]

One woman, now in her sixties, told us that as a teenager she read van de Velde and shared the information with her closest girlfriend. Instead of going to the movies on Saturday afternoon, they would sit at home exercising their PC muscles. "I'm doing it now," one would say to the other. "Are you?" This woman developed very strong PC muscles and became multiply orgasmic. She did not practice relaxing the muscle, however, and also developed occasional vaginismus.

As part of a routine gynecological examination, van de Velde gave his patients instruction in muscle exercise and urged that other gynecologists "use such inevitable professional occasions to be of help to their patients in this way as well."[7] Unfortunately, few gynecologists other than Kegel took his advice.

The avoidance of sexuality by the medical profession continued into the 1940s and 1950s, and greatly curtailed the potential impact of Arnold Kegel's work. Kegel had read van de

Velde and, in the late 1940s, confirmed and expanded his observations through the development of a complete "package" for restoration of the PC muscle. By 1952, he had sufficient clinical experience to convince him that his method worked and could drastically reduce the incidence of surgery for PC problems.

Kegel published a number of articles in the early 1950s in which he claimed to have successfully treated 86 percent of some 3,000 patients suffering from stress incontinence with his perineometer and exercise method.[8] He also noted that, in almost every instance, improvement in PC muscle strength and control brought spontaneous improvement in sexual response. Women often experienced orgasm for the first time.

Kegel, like Gräfenberg, was one of the losers in the intellectual power struggle that so often dominates scientific research circles. He never published after 1956, when the Kinsey and Masters and Johnson "clitoral only" school was in its ascendency, and only very recently have both Kegel and Gräfenberg been rediscovered.

Even today, although Kegel exercises are used around the world, they are seldom prescribed in America, except by childbirth educators.

> It is one of the mysteries of the history of sexual therapy that although "Kegel's exercises" are known and practiced throughout the world for the treatment of stress incontinence, the sexual aspects of this work have largely been ignored, even by such noted investigators as Kinsey and Masters and Johnson.[9]

It still seems tragic that the team that was to exert such a profound influence on contemporary sex research did not give appropriate recognition to Kegel's discoveries.

Not until 1979 was the first statistical and experimental evidence concerning the relationship between PC muscle strength and orgasmic capacity actually reported. In that year, Benjamin Graber, M.D., and Georgia Kline-Graber, R.N., a team of sex therapists, analyzed the data they had collected from 281 women who had visited their clinic. Patients were divided into three groups: those who could not achieve orgasm at all, those who could achieve orgasm with direct clitoral stimulation but not during intercourse, and those who could achieve orgasm *both* clitorally and during intercourse. As might be predicted, the group that could have orgasm with either clitoral or vaginal stimulation had the strongest muscles (with an average reading on Kegel's perineometer of 17), and those who could not achieve orgasm under any conditions had the weakest PC muscles (an average reading of 7). The middle group, which could achieve orgasm only with clitoral stimulation, was somewhere in between in terms of muscle strength (an average reading of 12). The authors concluded that "a major circumvaginal muscle is impaired in women who are unable to achieve orgasm."[10]

The Graber results are consistent with those of Perry and Whipple. Based on experiences with clinical patients while using the vaginal myograph, they reported that the stronger the muscles, the more likely those women were to experience orgasm as a result of vaginal stimulation. In another report, they observed that women who ejaculate during orgasm (at least once in a while) appeared to have significantly stronger PC muscle contractions than women who never ejaculated.[11]

At a recent biofeedback conference, during a seminar on physical therapy and muscles, the speaker, a woman with a national reputation, distributed a booklet picturing hundreds of individual muscles in great detail. After examining the illustrations, a participant asked, "Why is there a big blank circle on your diagram in the area below the navel and between the thighs?"

"Oh," replied the instructor, with obvious embarrassment, "to tell the truth, there are some very important muscles in the pelvis, but physical therapists traditionally don't pay any attention to them."

There are many reasons why other professionals, such as gynecologists and physical therapists, wanted as little contact as possible with the sexual muscles of their patients. The most obvious one is the fear of being accused of prurient interests. Unfortunately, our society often condones this stance to the detriment of our health. For example, most psychologists in America are enrolled in a malpractice insurance package offered through the American Psychological Association. There is one kind of "malpractice" case that is specifically excluded from that group policy: A suit for damages arising out of an alleged sexual relationship between therapist and patient. No wonder it is difficult to get professional help with problems involving the sexual muscles.

This situation is particularly unfortunate because most people have strong personal feelings associated with their sexual muscles. These are often more intense than feelings associated with the muscles in other parts of the body. When people begin to pay attention to their pelvic muscles, it often happens that intense feelings are triggered, together with the recall of significant interpersonal events. In Bioenergetic Analysis, this sort of recall frequently occurs in conjunction with the release of tension in other parts of the body as well.

Judy was in her forties when she began vaginal myography for stress incontinence. The more her muscles improved, the unhappier she became.

Finally, she stopped doing the exercises. Her thera-
pist suggested she consider the "advantages" of hav-
ing weak PC muscles. Before long, Judy came upon
an important insight. Several years earlier, she had
developed a crush on a man who worked in her
office. For months she sat at her typewriter day-
dreaming about him and squeezing her PC muscles.
One day Mr. Wonderful noticed Judy and began to
get friendlier. The friendlier he got, the more
frightened she became. Judy had enjoyed her fan-
tasies, but the possibility of an actual "affair" was
unthinkable. She began to associate contractions of
her PC muscle with immoral and dangerous feel-
ings. Several years after that unconsummated rela-
tionship, the same feelings of immorality and dan-
ger surfaced when Judy began to do her PC
exercises to correct her bladder problem.

Judy's story demonstrates the importance of understanding
the potential complications of PC muscle training. It is not
unusual for exercise to trigger old memories and fears that may
require professional counseling or at least the patient understanding of a good friend. Professionals who are involved and
experienced with muscle training should be able to detect and
handle "resistance." It is usually advisable to slow down the
muscle training and deal with the emotions it generates before
proceeding.

Another problem to be aware of when helping people train
their PC muscles is the ease with which people can associate
the newly found good feelings with the person who happens to
be there when they occur. In much the same way, it often happens that singers fall in love with their teachers. This occurs
because, in the process of opening up the throat, the pelvic area

also opens up, leading to deep sexual feelings. Singers sometimes believe that the good feelings they themselves have created by their own activity are due to the person who has helped them to use their muscles in a new way. The same thing can and does happen when helping someone learn to use their PC muscles. As in all types of therapeutic endeavor, therapists must be familiar with such phenomena and must be able to handle their own and their clients' emotional reactions with tact, understanding, and professional integrity.

At the beginning of our discussion of pelvic muscles, we mentioned another, deeper set of muscles that, like the inner third of the PC muscle, are innervated by the pelvic nerve. These are the muscles of the uterus. When Perry and Whipple were investigating the role of internal muscles in female ejaculation, they invented a uterine myograph which, like the cervical cap, fits directly over the cervix. EMG sensors are mounted in the rim of the cap, making it possible to investigate muscular activity of the uterus (without using the more invasive procedures developed by researchers in England[12]).

Using this device, Whipple and Perry discovered that two of the twenty women who participated in one of their research projects were able to *independently* contract either the PC muscle *or* the deeper uterine muscles. The other eighteen women always used both groups of muscles together.

The possibility of two independent internal muscle groups was fascinating because it helped explain the underlying mechanism of different kinds of orgasms as well as female ejaculation. Van de Velde had already stated this clearly in 1926: "Women must learn how to bring the muscles into play *separately*, and use them either simultaneously or in succession."[13]

The role of the external pelvic muscles, mentioned at the start of this chapter, is also important to sexual response. There is clinical evidence to support this, and the Ladas study,

"Women and Bioenergetic Analysis," supplies further confirmation.

There is also the anthropological evidence. For example, Malinowski described another string game that was played by the Trobriand Islanders and that illustrates the importance of free pelvic movement in both partners: "The strings are then pulled so that the center loop, which represents the genitals, moves rapidly up and down, and right and left, and this . . . stands for the characteristic motion in sexual congress."[14]

In "Movement and Feeling in Sex," psychiatrist Alexander Lowen wrote:

> Healthy sexual intercourse combines intense feelings and strong active movements . . . this is as true of the woman as of the man. In the act of coitus itself the feelings and movements are so fused . . . that the total act is a unity of emotional expression.[15]

Movement depends on muscles. The ability to move rhythmically and to sustain both voluntary and involuntary motion depends on muscle flexibility and strength. As with the PC, when the external muscles are too flaccid, they cannot function and they lose their sensitivity. When they are too tense, either chronically or situationally, they cannot move freely, and there is also a loss in sensitivity. According to Lowen, "kinesthetic pleasure," which becomes more important in the second phase of the sexual act, "depends upon the motility of the pelvis." (Lowen regards sensuous contact all over the body as essential to the first phase.) If the pelvis cannot swing freely, "like the free swing of a dangling leg," the tempo of pelvic movement cannot increase and sexual sensitivity is decreased.

There are several ways in which the motility of the pelvis can be blocked. Chronic tension can "unite the pelvis to the thighs below and to the lumbar spine above," forcing the person to move the whole body at once. This reduces sensation and curtails the movements necessary for pleasure and stimulation of the internal sexual organs. People compensate for this in a number of ways. Sometimes they tense the buttock muscles and push the pelvis instead of allowing a natural thrust to occur. Sometimes they pull the pelvis forward by tensing the abdominal muscles. According to Lowen, both maneuvers tend to interfere with the flow of feeling and the fullness of release.

Much the same thing can happen if the muscles become weak and flaccid or have atrophied from disuse, exactly like the PC muscle. With weak or atrophied muscles, it becomes difficult to move the pelvis at all, let alone for a sufficient amount of time.

Bodily mobility in general is impaired when the lower part of the body becomes dissociated from the upper part. Movements then become fragmented, and frequently the person separates sexuality from tender feelings, as the muscles function without a concomitant graceful integration. According to bioenergetic theory, whatever happens on a psychological level also occurs on a somatic (bodily) level.

The disturbances that occur in *involuntary* movements, which, when things are working well, occur at the peak of the sexual experience, parallel those that are found in voluntary movement. Muscles are not free to function involuntarily any differently than they can function voluntarily.

This is a brief summary of important ways in which the tone of the external muscles may affect sexual response in women and men. Women who answered the first questionnaire circulated by Alice and Harold Ladas reported that therapy had helped them to free tense muscles and to build up flaccid ones. Eighty-one percent of the women therapists reported that their experience of sexual climax improved in many significant ways after therapy. The importance of muscle tone is highlighted by the finding that the pelvis moved more freely for fifty-four percent of the respondents, and less voluntary effort was required for forty-three percent after therapy. This probably led to more effective stimulation of the G spot, as well as greater perception of sensation. One respondent described her experience this way:

> Before therapy I had just been dead. I really clamped down on those feelings and muscles. I'd always been constipated and found out how tight and tense I am in that whole area, or was, and how much anxiety I've experienced. I began to feel feelings that I never had before. I began to have a sex life and have orgasms, and it was just fantastic.

Another woman provided a more concrete illustration of the importance of stronger muscles:

> When I began to work bioenergetically, I could hardly hang on to a horse with my legs. Four years later, with no riding in between, it was easy for me to stay on using my legs. Also, from having no orgasms I became orgasmic with clitoral stimulation. Then I began to have vaginal orgasms in intercourse with clitoral stimulation, but without much movement involved. Now there's no clitoral stimulation required. When I let go, there's a melting in my vagina. It is a physical sensation, an "I love you" feeling, and it is vaginal. There is no tensing of muscles, and the feeling is not the same as letting the sensation build.

Other women said things like "I feel free to climax several times and to ask for cooperation from my partner," "there's more connection between my heart and genitals," and "it's a more intense total-body experience without interference from my mind."

Comments like "the orgasm moves up and down from head to toes" reflect an overall change in bodily mobility that depends not only on freeing and toning the pelvic muscles but on doing this with muscles *throughout the body*. The same thing is true of the comments concerning more connection between the heart and the genitals and less interference from the mind. When muscles in and around the neck and the chest and shoulders are freed, these things happen.

One therapist described the connection between freeing external pelvic musculature and other attitudes:

> At the beginning, many of the women did not know how to assert themselves and could not assert themselves in their lives because of the tension in their pelvises. But after therapy they began to report that their sex lives were improving, that they were having more frequent orgasms, and that they were more relaxed.

When working with people to help them release contracted pelvic muscles, or muscles in other parts of the body, some of the problems described in connection with training the PC muscle come into play and are often even more difficult to deal with. Pleasure anxiety is a reality. As one woman put it, "I got scared to death because there was no one to tell me that's what happens when you begin to unfreeze and to have all those marvelous feelings." Another said, "I think I had more sexual pleasure before therapy because I was more disassociated from that part of my body. As I connected with it in therapy, I felt more fear, more tension, and periods of frigidity. These were, however, transient problems."

Nevertheless, people can do a lot by themselves to develop, stretch, and exercise their external pelvic muscles as well as their PC muscle, often with considerable benefit to sexual functioning. Many cultures incorporate dances such as the hula or Middle Eastern or Oriental dancing into everyday activities in such a way that the pelvic muscles are identified, strengthened, and brought under control. Closer to home, disco dancing can also help these muscles.

At present, no one knows for sure whether training the external muscles has any effect on the condition of the PC, although we suspect that it does. What we do know is that when the pelvic muscles are strong and flexible enough to move freely, the G spot and the clitoris (or both) are more likely to be stimulated during intercourse. This was confirmed by the finding of the Ladases' second survey. The bioenergetic analysts and other professional therapists who responded to the questionnaire felt that the only other factors that are comparably important are the position used for intercourse and the depth of one's emotional involvement with one's partner.

Many of the women who participated in the Ladases' first study reported that they changed from experiencing climax only through clitoral stimulation to experiencing climax through vaginal penetration, without the need for clitoral stimulation:

> Before therapy, I had had intense sexual pleasure and orgasmic experience, but it was all clitorally oriented. After four years, I began to have vaginal orgasms. There wasn't any need for manual clitoral

stimulation, though there might have been clitoral stimulation in the process of intercourse. The orgasm was completely fulfilling, and I didn't feel I missed out on anything. But I wouldn't want to be told that now I couldn't have clitoral stimulation, because there are times when it's very pleasure-giving, and I want it. What is true now is that it isn't necessary for me to have clitoral stimulation in order to have orgasm.

This woman's remarks remind us that people experience more than one type of orgasm—and that they value the variety of sexual experience. They don't wish to relinquish one in favor of the other. This leads directly to chapter 5, "New Understandings of Human Orgasm."

·5·

New Understandings of Human Orgasm

In the realm of sexuality, pluralism is the essence of humanity. By taking diversity into account, we not only more nearly duplicate reality, we can also more appropriately serve our needs while cherishing the multifaceted wonders of our universe. Like snowflakes, human beings are all different. And so is our experience of orgasm.

There is, said biochemist Roger Williams, a "need in human biology and medicine for more attention to variability and individuality."[1] The Kinsey group recognized this in 1948 when they wrote "The living world is a continuum in each and every one of its aspects. The sooner we learn this concerning human sexual behavior, the sooner we shall reach a sound understanding of the realities of sex."[2]

Since that time, our understanding of the continuum of human sexual experience has been enlarged by the work of many sexologists. If we can forgo the temptation to look for the right way or the normal way or the healthy way, we may be able to help many more people enjoy their own particular experiences with increasing pleasure and satisfaction.

In at least two areas, dieting and sex, all "experts" claim to have the single best solution, and astonishing numbers of people pay heed to what they say. The truth is that there are many ways to enjoy sexuality, just as there are many ways to lose or gain weight or become healthier through changing our eating habits.

After Kinsey called attention to the clitoris as the main focus of sexual sensitivity in women, medical and laboratory studies concentrated on discovering the one universal mechanism of sexual response. When Masters and Johnson announced in 1966 that all orgasms were essentially the same, many people felt relieved and adopted an even more dogmatic version of that position than Masters and Johnson themselves.

It was not easy to disagree publicly with Masters and Johnson and their followers, so when Perry and Whipple gave a presentation at the 1980 meeting of the American Association of Sex Educators, Counselors and Therapists (AASECT), they put forward their theory of the "continuum of orgasm" with some trepidation. A few months later, at the November 1980 meeting of the Society for the Scientific Study of Sex (SSSS), the Ladases presented their view of a continuum of sexual responses. This was the original basis for our collaboration. The Ladases' study challenged another orthodoxy, the equally limited bioenergetic view about what orgasm should be: vaginally induced, involving the total body, and resulting in one, not multiple, climaxes.

Two factors had combined to deprive researchers of an objective viewpoint. Psychotherapists saw the damage suffered by women who were made to feel guilty, inferior, or downright immoral for enjoying their clitorises, while feminists felt that switching the focus of attention away from the vagina was one more valuable means of liberating women from excessive dependency upon men. In themselves, both were worthwhile observations, yet they became stumbling blocks for investigators seeking the truth about women's sexuality.

We prefer to follow Kinsey's advice and look at the experience of orgasm as part of several different continuums. One involves the place that triggers the response—in women, the Gräfenberg spot or clitoris; in men, the penis or prostate (and perhaps other places as well for both). A second concerns the type of response which results from that stimulation. Is the physiological activity always the same, or are there variations? Is there one climax or a series of them? Is the response sharply focused in the genitals or is it diffused throughout the entire body? Another continuum has to do with the feelings that accompany the experience; these may range from hatred and anger, to pain and revulsion, to love and ecstasy. Still another continuum takes into account the person or object with whom one is involved sexually. The gamut runs from autoeroticism, through objects and animals, to human beings of the same or the opposite sex. Special conditions may include the sharing of sex with one person or with many different people, or with persons of different ages, or body types, or physical characteristics. Another continuum concerns the purpose of sexual behavior, whether it is casual, recreational, or an expression of commitment. And there are other continuums as well. While all of these are extremely important dimensions of human sexuality, only three—what triggers the response, the effect of the response, and how much of the body is involved in it—lie within the scope of this book.

In chapter 2, we discussed the G spot and the fact that most women report that stimulation of the G spot feels quite different from stimulation of the clitoris. Prior to the pinpointing and naming of the G spot, it was difficult to discuss vaginal stimulation without sounding vague and sometimes mystical.

One woman who came in for sex therapy illustrates this problem well.

> *Susan, a minister's daughter, found it difficult to talk about her genitals without embarrassment. When her therapist described the newly discovered G spot, a smile came over her face. "That's very interesting," she said. "You know, for twenty-nine years we've had this problem, but I never felt right about bringing it up. Charles likes to stick his penis all the way inside me, but to tell the truth, I like it best when he's only about four inches in."*

Her preference, of course, was for the head of the penis to stimulate the G spot. Her husband, who was totally unaware of this area, thrust deeply every time. The therapist summarized their problem: Susan had been backing up at the rate of two inches per thrust for twenty-nine years! After they heard about the G spot, the couple found a new way to communicate about sexual pleasures and positions.

We have already mentioned the extent to which Masters and Johnson's assumption about the centrality of clitoral stimulation became, in the hands of popular writers, their "conclusion." In reality, Masters and Johnson accepted the Kinsey conclusion without fully investigating it. As recently as the 1981 annual meeting of AASECT, William Masters repeated once again his conviction that "all orgasms involve direct or indirect stimulation of the clitoris."

We do not agree. We have begun to study reports from women who utilize the perineal area as an additional locus of

sexual stimulation—which can evoke orgasm. Although both
the perineum and the clitoris are both connected to the pudendal nerve, most women can clearly distinguish between stimulation of the two. As with the G spot, it often takes several
minutes of initial stimulation before the mental interpretation
becomes clearly positive. Like the "bladder-signal" reaction to
G spot contact, most women have nonsexual associations with
the perineum which have to be overcome before they can
enjoy its intrinsic sexual pleasure. (Because stimulation of the
perineum may be an important sexual experience for some
women, physicians should think twice before doing routine
episiotomies, a cut into the perineum that facilitates passage of
the baby's head during the final stages of birth.)

Another interesting variation on the clitoris-only theory is
the approach taken in *A New View of a Woman's Body*. The
authors were dismayed by the usual description of the clitoris
as a tiny bud situated some distance from the vagina, and
invented a new vocabulary in which various adjacent parts,
once known only by medical names, are described as compris-
ing the "whole" clitoris, in its broadest and most inclusive
sense. As mentioned earlier, the area which we have termed
the G spot became the "urethral sponge of the clitoris." It is
not clear if this "new view of the clitoris" will have any influence in medical circles, but it certainly does broaden the focus
beyond the tiny organ stroked with Kinsey's Q-tip-like devices.

Even in its traditional, limited formulation, the clitoris is
more complicated than most researchers have acknowledged.
A glance at any standard anatomy text reveals that in addition
to the primary nerve connections that the tip or glans of the
clitoris has with the pudendal nerve, the shaft and its attach-
ments are believed to be connected to the pelvic nerve deeper
inside the body. This fact, often overlooked by sex researchers,

has important implications and helps to explain the tremendous variety of response patterns that different women enjoy.

Most medical texts give more attention to descriptions of the penis than they do to the clitoris, but the quality of that attention is just as limited. Few people attempt to explain the nature of male stimulation beyond the "sensitivity" of the glans of the penis and, occasionally, the underside of the shaft. Almost no mention is ever made—in scientific publications at least—of the sexual sensitivity of the male prostate gland. Adopting the rationale discussed above, this organ would have to be rechristened "the urethral sponge of the penis" to take into account its significant location exactly at the base of the penile shaft, a fact that is often overlooked except when the gland becomes irritated or infected and requires medical attention. The situation is quite different, however, in pornographic literature, where the sensitivity of the male prostate has often been described in terms reminiscent of the G spot. One cannot help but be struck by the similarity between descriptions of prostate stimulation and reports from women upon discovering their G spot. This is not surprising, since both appear to be evolutionary descendants of the same tissue.

The implication that prostate sensitivity plays a significant role in male sexual response may strike many readers as odd. Indeed, many men are only aware of negative associations with their prostate gland, sometimes derived from the unpleasant experience of a rectal examination by their physicians. Because of this, as well as our negative associations with feces and the anus, most Western men have never considered the prostate part of their sexual apparatus, although it does account for the frequency with which men experience sexual dysfunctions as a result of prostate surgery (just as the area of the G spot has often been damaged during surgical procedures).

Consider, for example, the experience of this male psychologist:

While listening to women describe their experiences with G spot stimulation, he became quite confused by their insistence that there was a precise "spot" that, when they touched it, felt distinctly better than the rest of the upper vaginal wall.

"Well," said a nurse. "Have you ever had your prostate examined?"

"No," he admitted. So she instructed him to lie down, and inserted a lubricated finger. "Yee-ow-ow!" he screamed, as she quickly located his virgin prostate.

He described the sensation as a stabbing pain and was convinced that his prostate had been pierced by a long fingernail. He demanded to inspect the nurse's finger, and was shocked to discover that she had hardly any fingernails at all.

"How could I have been so wrong?" he asked himself. As a psychologist, he knew the answer: body sensations—or, more precisely, their interpretation by the human brain—are always "learned." He asked the nurse to repeat the procedure. This time the results were distinctly different. There was no sharp pain, nor even any dull pain. Although the idea of a finger poking into his anus was "weird," he had to admit that it felt good. Indeed, very quickly it began to feel terrific.

He later commented on what the experience had taught him. When the prostate was touched, he was able to isolate sensations associated with a familiar sexual experience—ejaculation. He discovered that

*the prostate had been familiar to him all along as
"the base of my penis," which always throbbed during an ejaculatory orgasm.*

His observations led us to examine the role of the prostate in
male sexual functioning. They also added further evidence to
the notion that, all things considered, men and women are
more alike than previously assumed.

After Perry and Whipple began discussing the role of prostatic stimulation in scientific forums, a number of gay men
agreed that the authors were "right on target." Although it is
seldom discussed openly, the primary reward of the "receptive" role in male anal intercourse is direct penile stimulation
of the recipient's prostate gland. Curiously enough, here is
another parallel between men and women. The same "doggie
position" that Elaine Morgan describes as facilitating penile
contact with the "ventral wall" of the vagina (i.e. the G spot)
also facilitates contact with the male prostate. In fact, one of
the reasons some men may enjoy homosexual relationships is
that they often provide more frequent stimulation of the prostate than heterosexual involvements. (It is an interesting parallel that, initially, a lesbian community in Miami had a great
influence on Perry and Whipple's research about female ejaculation and the location of the G spot.)

The findings published by Perry and Whipple in 1980 were
unique in identifying more than one place in the vagina where
female orgasm can occur. Previous research, such as that of
Masters and Johnson, had the objective of finding the "essential" aspects that were common to all sexual orgasms. In
attempting to isolate these common factors, they necessarily
overlooked a great deal that did not fit the pattern, and so they
discarded a lot of information that did not fit their initial
assumptions (such as the opportunity to investigate women who

masturbated without touching their clitorises).[3] This helped them find what they were looking for: a pattern common to all the women they studied. But they were not in a position to generalize from that result to the rest of womankind, since their sample was biased.

Most of the people who read the reports of Masters and Johnson made the mistake of interpreting their results to mean that Masters and Johnson had "discovered" or "proved" that "all orgasms are the same."[4] In actuality, the unitary nature of orgasm was not a "finding" but an "assumption."

Since Kinsey's publications appeared, men and women have begun to act in accordance with the official information, which was rapidly incorporated into popular literature. Ironically, better educated people with greater access to printed information were more influenced by the doctrine that all orgasms are the same and result from clitoral stimulation.

Irving Singer, Ph.D., professor of philosophy at MIT, noted that Kinsey distinguished between two contrasting "systems of mores."[5] Kinsey described one pattern involving "prolonged pre-coital play, a considerable variety in techniques, a maximum of stimulation before coital union, some delay after effecting such union, and finally, orgasm which is simultaneous for the male and female."[6] Except for the last element, this also describes the single ideal advanced by Masters and Johnson's sexual therapy.

By contrast, there is another "system" involving simple and direct intercourse, an alternative that is at once sanctioned by Anglo-American law, ridiculed as "Wham, bam, thank you, ma'am," and, nevertheless, commonly practiced among the working classes and the less educated. As Singer pointed out, people who favor this kind of sex were systematically excluded from Masters and Johnson's research population, which included mostly college-educated women. One reason for the wide variety of responses in the letters about G spot stimulation and female ejaculation included in this book may be the diverse backgrounds of women who wrote them.

There were some vocal intellectuals, though, who also happened to prefer "simple and direct" intercourse. After some ten years of silence following the publication of Masters and Johnson's work, they began to assert themselves and protest that, in spite of the official theory, they experienced sex differently. For example, one woman psychologist wrote: "I have frequently found assertions in professional literature which contradicted my own experience, and provided no help in understanding it." The woman was the daughter of an anthropologist who was interested in comparative sexual mores, and she grew up looking forward to the coitally oriented sex that is typical in many other cultures. Only years later did she learn to manipulate her clitoris directly, and while she sometimes does so, she still prefers the distinctly different orgasm which results from intercourse.

Women who insist that all orgasms are the same are probably (1) telling the truth—about themselves, and (2) wrong—about people in general. Only women who are able to experience two different kinds of orgasm can help settle the question. Fortunately, such women are beginning to make themselves heard. For instance, one woman wrote to us:

> I most certainly have two very different types of climax. One is from direct stimulation of the clitoris and surrounding area. It seems to come about quickly and is not as intense or long-lasting. The other climax is produced through intercourse. I refer to it as an "inner climax." I get the best inner climax with the man on the top, me lying down. Another position that brings about inner climax

very quickly is with the man on a chair and me sitting on him, facing each other.

Other women find that they experience this kind of climax more easily or only when on top of their partners. One wrote to say that she "has always enjoyed sex more when she was on top because it was so much easier (and better!) to have an orgasm that way."

Another woman said:

I have long experienced two distinct types of orgasm, and I learned the difference after having clitoral orgasm through the use of a vibrator. Before that I experienced pleasure and satisfaction from intercourse, but I always wondered if there might not be something else. Since discovering that I have the capability of experiencing two very different but equally pleasurable types of orgasms, my feelings about my own sexuality have been greatly enhanced. Your research should be continued for the benefit of those who still are not aware or for those, like me, who will be grateful for professional acknowledgment of something they have in fact known about for a long time.

It seems to be a two-way street. Ironically, we were better prepared to believe the reports of women who claimed to experience two kinds of orgasm, because of the evidence in our laboratory that supported their views.

The late humanist psychologist, Abraham Maslow, Ph.D., argued that too many theories were spawned by the study of "sick people," i.e. mental patients. He suggested that theorists should instead study the most self-motivated and self-validating people, whom he called "self-actualized." In 1978, Perry decided to apply a similar strategy to sex research when he attempted to replicate Masters and Johnson's muscle contraction data with laboratory subjects. He asked male college students who the "sexiest" women on campus were. Several names kept reappearing, so he invited the unknowing "winners" to become paid research subjects, and one consented.

On a written test of sexual interest, she received the highest possible score. She also demonstrated good control over her PC muscle, which was quite strong. At first, during masturbation, her PC muscle showed normal, expected increases in tension. But as she became more aroused, suddenly PC muscle activity ceased. The laboratory technicians assumed that their research subject was taking a break—until the remote signal light flashed that the woman was having an orgasm.

When we talked with her later, she assured us that she knew what an orgasm was and that she had had a perfectly normal one. Was she wrong, was she lying, or had she experienced some "other kind" of orgasm from the type which Masters and Johnson had described and defined as "normal"? After all, she had been selected not for being normal, but "supernormal."

Perry was baffled. He had read about the Singer theory, which describes "three types of orgasm": "vulval," corresponding to Masters and Johnson's unitary type; "uterine," which involves cervical jostling; and "blended," which includes elements of both. But, like other researchers at the time, he was unwilling to believe anyone who criticized Masters and Johnson, and it wasn't until he joined Whipple in 1979 in a study of "female ejaculation" that the possibility of other kinds of orgasm began to make sense.

Most women who ejaculate state that their ejaculatory orgasms feel quite different from orgasms induced by clitoral stimulation. There are, to be sure, a great variety of orgasmic styles among ejaculators, and a small minority, perhaps ten percent, insist that they only ejaculate upon oral stimulation of their clitoris. (The proximity of a partner's face to the ejaculation from the urethra was usually responsible for their first becoming aware that they had ejaculated.) Another larger group reports that they only ejaculate during exceptionally passionate intercourse. While they seldom offer firsthand reports about the source of the ejaculation, their experience fits in with the Singer theory of "uterine" or deeper orgasms induced by "cervical jostling."

The most helpful group in terms of formulating a new theory of vaginal sensitivity has been those women, lesbian and straight, who insist they they usually or only ejaculate in response to direct stimulation of their G spot by their partner's fingers. As mentioned earlier, not only were such women initially responsible for focusing our attention on the spot itself as a center of sexual arousal distinct from the clitoris, but they also provided the first clear evidence that the "spot" tends to swell as sexual stimulation continues. Finally, these women reported that at the moment of ejaculatory orgasm, the vagina underwent a dramatic transformation.

Two phenomena were consistently observed. First, there is no formation of an "orgasmic platform," or constricted vaginal entrance, which is characteristic of the orgasm described by Masters and Johnson. These women reported that instead of constricting, the vaginal musculature relaxes and the entrance opens. (It is possible that the orgasmic platform is formed, at least in the sense that there is some swelling of the tissues at the entrance to the vagina, but that the effect of relaxation of the PC muscle and the expansion of the entrance is so great as to nullify or at least obscure that swelling.)

Second, and even more dramatic, is the absence of a "tenting effect" like that described by Masters and Johnson, which occurs during clitorally induced climaxes when the inner portion of the vagina often balloons as a result of the lifting up of the uterus inside the abdomen. Sometimes during this type of orgasm the PC muscle becomes exceedingly tight, while the inner portion of the vagina expands so much that all contact with the penis is lost. (Again, the effect is more apparent to a probing finger.) Although Masters and Johnson named this the "tenting effect," what they were describing really resembles an inverted tent.

Quite the opposite reaction is often felt during ejaculatory orgasm. Instead of pulling up and expanding the inner portion of the vagina, the uterus seems to be pushed down and the upper portion of the vagina compresses. Many ejaculatory women describe something like the Valsalva maneuver, the downward pressure associated with emptying the bowels. Perry and Whipple coined the term "A-Frame-effect" to distinguish it from the inverted "tenting effect," and to provide a clear symbol of the difference. Many ejaculators report that the hand that is stimulating the G spot is often pushed out of the vagina by the downward pressure of the internal organs. We have also been told that the penis is sometimes pushed out of the vagina during such orgasms. One man reported that he had experienced this type of response, and that he had not only been ejected, but had also felt dejected: "It was unpleasant to suddenly find myself out in the cold at the moment of her orgasm, and it was difficult for her too. At first I thought my penis was too small, but then I learned to enjoy her pleasure from this type of response."

The A-Frame effect is not unique to ejaculatory orgasms, however. One non-ejaculator described her two kinds of masturbatory orgasms as follows:

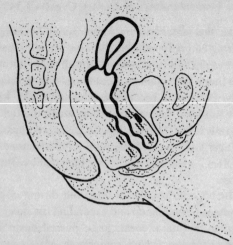

(Inverted) Tenting effect described by Masters and Johnson

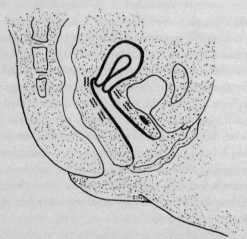

A-Frame effect described by Perry and Whipple

Illustration 6

> *I have two vibrators. I use one for one kind of orgasm, and the second for the other. When I want to have a regular "clitoral" orgasm, I stimulate my clitoris and labia with a large plug-in model that really hums. But sometimes I want the other kind. I have a small, bullet-shaped vibrator which is only about four inches long, and it slips completely inside the vagina. It tickles my G spot, and when I come that way my little vibrator is expelled like a missile!*

As we pieced together the evidence that suggested there might be more than one kind of orgasm, we had several blocks of data to incorporate. First, there were the subjective reports of many women and men who insisted that they had experienced at least two different "kinds" of orgasm. Many of them claimed that these two kinds were associated with stimulation of different genital areas. Second, there was our own laboratory evidence that some women achieved what they claimed were satisfying orgasms *without* the characteristic contractions of the orgasmic platform. And, third, we were confronted with the undeniable fact of female ejaculation, especially in response to G spot stimulation. A cursory examination of any anatomy text shows that there is no direct neural pathway from the G spot to the pudendal nerve, nor from the pudendal nerve to the uterus and other internal organs. Since the G spot is connected to the spinal cord through the pelvic nerve, which also serves the bladder and uterus, we concluded that this must be the pathway involved in ejaculatory and other "inner" orgasms.

Our focus on the pelvic nerve provided answers to other questions as well. The pelvic nerve is one of the most complex in the human body, and a major branch, called the hypogastric plexus, extends upward from the internal organs to the middle portion of the spinal cord. The route of the hypogastric plexus suggests a connection between pelvic muscle activity and breathing interruption (apnea), which Josephine and Irving Singer have described as a typical characteristic of what they called "uterine" orgasms.[7]

The activity of the pelvic nerve also provides an explanation for the sexual experiences of people who have suffered injuries to the lower segments of the spinal cord. If only the pudendal nerve were involved in transmitting sexual sensations, we would expect these people to have a total absence of sexual sensations, yet this is not true, and the hypogastric plexus may serve as their sexual nerve channel. A graduate student in her early thirties wrote:

> I am a paraplegic from the breastline down because of a spinal cord injury. Research about the Gräfenberg spot is of special interest to me, since it helps describe my orgasm, and I have always been told by doctors that I was not capable of experiencing a "normal" orgasm.

The importance of both the pelvic and pudendal nerves to sexual function has also received independent confirmation from several other researchers around the world.[8]

Perry and Whipple invented the uterine myograph to complement the vaginal myograph described in chapter 4 and to permit simultaneous measurement of both PC and uterine muscle contractions. In contrast to the single internal electrode employed by previous researchers, which was unable to determine the direction from which muscle signals emanated, their method placed a total of six EMG electrodes inside the vagina.

Three, on the vaginal myograph, were situated directly over the orgasmic platform or PC muscle. Three additional electrodes were affixed by the suction of the uterine myograph to the cervix itself. A single electrode would be equally sensitive to muscle signals from the vaginal entrance or from the deepest end of the vagina, and could not tell which is which. It would be like listening to a stereophonic recording with mono earphones. You could hear all the notes, but you couldn't determine which direction they were coming from.

Pilot research conducted with this combination of six sensors yielded promising results. In one experiment, intensive stimulation of the tip of the clitoris with a vibrator led to twice as much muscle activity in the PC as in the uterus, whereas slower, manual stimulation of the clitoris produced the opposite result.[9] Slower stimulation may have more effect on the shaft and base of the clitoris, which are connected to the pelvic nerve, while the pudendal nerve may be more responsive to stimulation of the tip of the clitoris. These results are consistent with our "two-nerve theory."

In another study, Perry and Whipple observed a research subject who claimed to regularly experience two kinds of orgasm, a "superficial" one brought about by clitoral stimulation, and a deeper, uterine orgasm achieved only through intercourse "when the emotional tie is great." Clitoral masturbation showed a modest response at the cervix (10) but G spot stimulation registered an orgasmic response of 14 microvolts.[10]

After reviewing the Singers' three categories and the experimental evidence, Perry and Whipple proposed an alternative schema in which female orgasms were represented by a continuum. At one end were the "outer" or clitorally induced orgasms, which mostly involve PC muscle activity, at the other end, the "deeper" or "uterine" orgasms described by Singer. The following chart incorporates both theories:

The Perry and Whipple continuum of orgasmic response

Reference:	1----2----3----4----5----6----7----8----9----10		
Singer's categories	Vulval orgasm	Blended orgasm	Uterine orgasm
Focus of muscle response	PC muscle	Both	Uterus
Common trigger point	Clitoris	Several	G spot
Major nerve involved	Pudendal nerve	Both	Pelvic nerve and hypogastric plexus
Number of orgasms	One or multiple	One or multiple	One: Terminative
Experience focus	Orgasmic platform	Vaginal	Uterus and pelvic organs
Male counterpart	Orgasm without semen expulsion	Typical ejaculatory orgasm	Non-ejaculatory emission
Common names	Clitoral orgasm	Vaginal orgasm	Vaginal orgasm

The column on the left refers to the "vulval" orgasm described by Masters and Johnson. It is referred to as "clitoral" by the Freudians because the clitoris is the common trigger point for stimulation. The most obvious manifestation of sexual response is in the rhythmic contractions of the PC muscle.[11]

To the person who experiences it, this orgasm appears to be focused in the surface genitals, or just below the surface. The extent to which the entire body responds is an entirely separate continuum. It can range from very slight clonic contractions localized in the genitals to vibrations in every muscle of the body. More typically, however, it is fairly localized. Orgasms like this are readily produced by vibrator stimulation in some women:

> *One research subject masturbated with her own vibrator while her PC muscle was being monitored by vaginal myography. During one hour we recorded some 70 discrete climaxes, consisting of 6 to 12 contractions of the PC in the form described by Masters and Johnson. The subject reported that at home she sometimes had 200 such climaxes in an hour—but that they were not very satisfying emotionally.*

At the other end of the continuum are those orgasms described by Singer as "uterine," or by others as "deep." Some "vaginal" orgasms might fit this category, but you will notice that the term *vaginal* also refers to the middle column. While this blended orgasm almost always occurs in response to penile thrusting during intercourse, it has also been observed to occur in response to direct manual stimulation of the G spot, especially in women who ejaculate.

We have speculated that the G spot is the nerve center or focal point of stimulation for this kind of orgasm, and that the pelvic nerve and hypogastric plexus provide the major nerve pathways. Response is typically felt to occur in the uterus, although adjacent pelvic structures (the upper vagina, the bladder, and supporting structures and muscles) may also be involved, especially when ejaculation occurs.

Women who have gone through labor are more likely to identify this type of orgasm as one of their experiences than women who have not.[12] Since many women first develop a clear sensory awareness of their own uterus only after becoming pregnant, this relationship is not surprising. We have also interviewed women who have had hysterectomies and who describe the orgasm as occurring in the place where their uterus "used to be."

Singer describes the "uterine" orgasm as usually satiating or terminative. That is, once you have had one, you just don't want or need another for many hours. Julian Davidson, Ph.D., of Stanford University, who developed a "bipolar hypothesis" of human sexuality, which complements our continuum theory, postulated that a muscular mechanism of satiation may be triggered by this kind of orgasm.[13] However, in view of the evidence that most human sexual behavior is learned rather than governed by hormones or other physiological factors, Perry and Whipple suggest that the terminative nature of some orgasms may be a learned behavior as well. This is especially likely in view of the evidence from ejaculators, some of whom have what can be described as "multiple ejaculatory orgasms," sometimes lasting up to an hour or more, in response to continuous G spot stimulation.

Referring back to the chart, while we are able, theoretically, to describe "pure" cases of the two ends of the orgasmic continuum, vulval (Reference 1) and uterine (Reference 10), we believe that, most of the time, most people experience orgasm somewhere in between these extremes. That is, *most* orgasms are "blended," and may be situated at any point along the orgasmic continuum. For instance, an orgasm that was theoretically plotted at Reference 3 on the continuum would involve much more clitoral stimulation than one that was plotted at Reference 6. The fact that the clitoral shaft is often stimulated during intercourse, as Masters and Johnson pointed out, adds credence to the concept of a blended orgasm. The pudendal and pelvic nerves interconnect at the spinal cord as well as several other places, offering the possibility that sexual stimulation of one nerve can be "blended" into the other area, which suggests another explanation for blended orgasms.

Supporting evidence also comes from the second Ladas study. Over three-quarters of the respondents reported experiencing more than one type of orgasm, over one-quarter more than one type of vaginal orgasm.

The chart of orgasmic responses mainly refers to the female orgasm, but we have included the male counterparts as well. Males differ anatomically from females, internally, only in the absence of the uterus and related reproductive organs. Their basic innervation and musculature is identical to that of the female, with obvious differences in the external organs.

Our initial impression is that most males learn very quickly to have "blended" or typical male ejaculatory orgasms. It may seem that the capacity for ejaculatory orgasm is simply biologically given, but that theory ignores considerable evidence that most males are actively *taught*, often by their peers, how to masturbate to orgasm. Whether it happens in "circle jerks" or through the exchange of schoolyard information, most adolescent males learn that it is manly to emit fluid, and more manly to emit more fluid farther.

Although most men are trained to think that the only real orgasm consists of a spurt of ejaculatory fluid, others have begun to experiment and have cultivated the orgasm without semen expulsion that corresponds to the female "vulval" orgasm and includes contractions of the PC muscle. Others have championed the nonconvulsive, deeper orgasm, which seems to involve internal contractions (mediated by the pelvic nerve) with some dribbling of semen. Obviously, we believe that no one way is right for either men or women. However, if the advocates of one or another kind of orgasm educate men and women to realize that a variety of alternatives is open to them, that would be a useful service.

A good case in point is the multiple orgasm. Since Masters and Johnson have shown that at least "vulval" orgasms, which they studied, could and did occur a great many times in a single sexual session, most authorities have taken the position that multiple orgasms are *theoretically* possible for all women.

Bioenergetic theory claims that multiple climaxes are superficial and unrewarding—the result of an inability to contain excitement and let it build to a full orgasm.[14] Nevertheless, women who took part in the Ladases' first study reported that 72 percent experienced multiple climax, and of those women 75 percent claimed that the experiences were orgasmic in nature, and 42 percent believed that Bioenergetic Analysis had improved their experience of multiple climax. Their statements about multiple climax contradicted official bioenergetic doctrine, and, until Perry and Whipple's theory became known, it was difficult to explain why. Looking at their continuum of orgasmic response, you can see that multiple orgasms often occur with blended orgasms, and not just with clitoral orgasms.

Although it had been shown that women could have multiple climaxes, it was assumed that men were incapable of this. Recently, however, reports have indicated that multiple orgasms are indeed possible for men,[15] and some men have indicated that they experience most satisfaction from a series of "deeper" orgasms culminating in a final, ejaculatory spurt. There are essential prerequisites: a healthy PC muscle, and the belief that you don't have to quit after the first one. It also helps if you are in good physical shape.

One remarkable thing about the results of recent research in sexuality is that we have been able to increase our understanding of one sex from studying the other. Our knowledge of the male prostate gland served to illuminate reports about the sensitive area in females that we have called the G spot. Our understanding of the sexual aspect of G spot stimulation in turn suggested that we reexamine the pleasure functions of the male prostate.

One more way in which women and men are more alike than different has to do with the extent to which the entire body is involved in orgasm. In traditional sexology, the words *climax* and *orgasm* are customarily used interchangeably, and no distinction is made between them. This ignores the possibility of another important continuum of sexual response, which stretches from climax to orgasm.

Wilhelm Reich drew a distinction between *climax*, a localized genital experience, and *orgasm*, in which the muscles of the entire body participate, not just the pelvis. A twenty-two-year-old woman who came for counseling described the contrast very vividly:

> I don't really enjoy sex with Clifford because I can't feel what he is experiencing. At the moment of greatest excitement, when he comes, he makes no sound. I can't feel or hear him breathing, and whatever happens occurs only in his penis. It embarrasses me that, by contrast, I make a lot of noise and my whole body moves in and out like an accordion. This feels good to me, but I don't feel a sufficient connection with him.

If you don't involve the whole body, said Reich, then you don't have a complete release, and that dammed-up energy seeks outlets in other, often destructive ways.[16]

One man who came for Bioenergetic Analysis reported that he got a blinding headache every time he had sex. That same man developed headaches while listening to opera because the sound of the human voice evoked such a strong reaction in him that his whole body would "vibrate" (his word). Once the tension in the occipital region had been released through therapy, he was able to enjoy both lovemaking and opera.

"Vibration," as the man called it, is another concept that does not appear in sexology literature, although poetry and love stories abound with references to it. In *The Way to Vibrant Health,* Alexander and Leslie Lowen wrote that "vibration is the key to aliveness.... A healthy body is in a constant state of vibration whether awake or asleep.... A living body is in constant motion; only in death is it truly still."[17]

One woman wrote:

> *I find it extremely important to have my legs free during sex ... they must be free in order for me to fully reach an orgasm. Once climax is reached my legs need to be free to vibrate to let the orgasm take place. If my legs are held, my upper body will shake and the climax is not as intense or as pleasurable.*

Lowen added that pleasure is related to the amount of tender or "heart" feelings. As one man put it: "Climax is a relief of sexual tension, orgasm more a deep satisfaction that I can only experience when my heart is involved."

Satisfaction, however, wrote Lowen, is a different dimension from pleasure and depends on the fullness of release.[18] If it occurs only in the genitals or pelvis, rather than throughout the body, and if release is only partial due to chronic muscle spasms, then satisfaction will be less complete.

Asked if she differentiated between climax and orgasm, one woman wrote:

> *Climax—feeling is limited to the genital area, clitoral origin, feels great there but not satisfying else-*

*where. Orgasm—feeling starts deep inside, flows
out to head, hands and feet, including entire body
at best of times and often stimulates deep, loving
feeling from heart or sad feelings (joy or tears
result).*

Here is what some other women and men had to say:

*Climax is in the vagina with contractions in the
abdomen and a deep, hot discharge of liquid.
Orgasm goes through the rest of the body
upwards—a sweet, yielding softness. I feel like
honey all over and enjoy it emotionally, mentally,
and physically.*

*Climax is the genital sensation in the penis.
Orgasm is a larger reaction involving the whole
organism.*

*Climax—the pinnacle of sexual excitement up
until orgasm. Orgasm—the streaming sensation
that continues after climax.*

*Climax does not leave me satisfied; orgasm pro-
vides a feeling of release.*

*I am more aware of orgasm moving up and down
my body and no longer try to stop that from happening.*

In other words, what many people refer to as "not a very good
orgasm" is what the people quoted above are calling a climax.
Out of 131 respondents to Alice Ladas's second question-

naire, about 60 made a distinction between climax and orgasm. Of these, approximately 90 percent specified that orgasm involves involuntary contractions over the entire body, that the heart is more involved, and the breathing is deeper. Eighty percent indicated that involuntary sounds occur.

In order to allow the entire body to become involved in clonic contraction and energy release, not only is it necessary to be free of chronically contracted or flaccid muscles and to be able to breathe freely, it is also helpful to feel comfortable about making sounds during the sexual act. That kind of abandon is easier to achieve as one becomes less shy with a partner and more experienced with one's own body.

Perry and Whipple's two-nerve theory may explain how a climax that involves the upper third of the PC muscle and the uterus is communicated, via the pelvic nerve, to other parts of the body and may partially account for the distinctions these men and women made between climax and orgasm. Respondents in the Ladas study indicate that the additional body sensations add to their pleasure, making relationships more meaningful, fulfilling, and tension-reducing.

More investigation with groups not already acquainted with Reich and Lowen's work is needed to further clarify the distinction between climax and orgasm, as well as the ways in which this is related to the two-nerve theory. For now, it is clear that many women and men are aware of this distinction, finding what they describe as orgasm to be more satisfying than the localized climax.

So we have several continuums of orgasmic experience. Inevitably some people are going to decide that they prefer orgasms that can be classified at one point or another on each continuum. We make no value judgment about where people are or want to be on these continuums. We do want people to be aware of their options and the various means of achieving them. As we have said before—but it is certainly important enough to repeat several times—don't use the information in this book to set up new standards for yourself or your partner because, by doing so, you may undermine the pleasures that are already yours.

·6·

The Best Is the Enemy of the Good

By now you have read a lot of new material about the physical aspects of human sexuality. Learning about these discoveries may have affected you in any number of ways. Like this thirty-six-year-old woman from Missouri, married to the same man for fourteen years, you may have felt relieved:

> I have felt weird because I do ejaculate a fluid during sex, during both foreplay and intercourse. I must have a towel under myself. The fluid is not urine, because sometimes after sex I have to go to the bathroom. The fluid has almost no odor and is clear. I do feel the spot of which you spoke, and my husband does find it by my responses. I just had to write to tell you that I now know there are other women who are like me. Thank you for helping me to feel better about myself. I have read books but have never found my "problem" in any of them.

A twenty-eight-year-old woman from Massachusetts who had a similar reaction sent five pages of personal history. Here is some of it:

> *At four I started using a toy bear with a bulbous nose to stimulate the spot. My mother found me under the sheet . . . and I never saw the bear again. At six, I started to play with my clitoris but never was entirely satisfied with the feeling it gave me, although it was pleasant. When I began to compare myself with my teenaged girlfriends, I realized that I was different. During my late teens, I had a steady boyfriend. Our sex was a weekend occurrence in the back seat of a car after my mother went to her hair appointments on Saturday mornings. He found a way to hit my "special spot," and I learned to have multiple orgasms this way. Then I read Kinsey and Masters and Johnson and tried to learn to respond clitorally, but I couldn't. Then, at twenty-two, I began to notice all that fluid. Now I was absolutely sure without a shadow of doubt: I was not normal. Then along came the Hite Report and it confirmed the facts I hated to realize. I didn't even think like an average woman. I thought like a man, despite the fact that I am most feminine. I felt that I must be a hermaphrodite. Although I tried not to let it bother me, I became even more aware of my "problem" when I had sex for the first time with my husband. He was dumbfounded when I reached my climax before him, and my vagina literally pushed him out. I am relating the events in my life hoping that in the future some poor girl like myself will be spared the despair and the hopeless feeling of self-*

alienation, of being different and not in the "normal" category. Thank God for your findings.

A woman from Alabama who wrote to us related:

> After I was married a few months, at age nineteen, I had my first "terrible" experience of a liquid orgasm. I thought I was urinating when this happened, and twenty-one years later I was still feeling I was some kind of freak.
>
> I would and do get this full feeling and pressure, and I need to push, and during this a very hot liquid is discharged. Being an avid reader, I have been searching all these years to discover anything like what I experience, with no luck. I have often wanted my husband to read some books on intercourse and loving but would never give him these, as it always mentions the contractions a woman has during orgasm. He has had (off and on) premature ejaculation, and I wanted him to read up on this to see that he was not a bad lover and that this happens sometimes. I could not let him, however, because I thought he would read about female orgasm and discover that I was not having an orgasm but urinating, and I would die of shame if he thought that. You see, all these years he has been thrilled if and when I have "an orgasm," because I guess he thinks this is the way a woman is—but I knew differently.
>
> But now I am very lighthearted to think I may be quite normal, and maybe I can relax and enjoy my husband instead of holding back these intense feelings I have when I feel so full and delightful.

You cannot imagine how your information has made me feel. I really feel free and think I can relax and maybe express myself more now.

Instead of feeling relief, perhaps you were excited, like this twenty-seven-year-old man from Wyoming, and eager to explore new pleasures with your partner!

When we first heard about female ejaculation, my wife had reached orgasm only through stimulation of her clitoris orally or manually. One month later, after we began experimenting, with Joanna in the top position, she expressed a lot of fluid which was milky in appearance. I kept reassuring her and encouraging her to enjoy herself, and she began to be much more responsive during intercourse.

A woman who has lived for fifteen years with the same female partner reacted in a similar fashion:

Suzanne and I were extremely interested in what you had to say about the Gräfenberg spot, and we have found great new enjoyment in helping each other to stimulate that spot. We have become much bolder about using our fingers inside of each other's vaginas.

From Arizona, a man of forty-eight wrote us:

It was such a help to learn about the G spot. Dana has never liked me to play with her clitoris, and that's all I ever learned about through reading. When we discovered how to find the G spot, we

*began to experiment and our sex life has become as
exciting again as it was when we were first married.*

A twenty-seven-year-old woman from Iowa with four children wrote to say:

*It is wonderful to know you are normal. For a lot of
years I thought to myself . . . is this all there is to
sex? But I was enlightened to discover that I have
that spot you were talking about! I'm thrilled to
know that there is so much more to sex than what
my mom told me.*

Perhaps you were neither excited nor relieved, but discovered, like this woman from South Carolina, that your pubococcygeus muscle was not in good shape and, using our material,
you put yourself through a course of PC muscle exercises:

*When I learned about the importance of muscle
tone, I began to think about my own history . . . the
difficult second childbirth and the fact that I have
been leaking urine ever since when I laugh or cough.
Thanks to your excellent instruction, I began to do
the PC exercises on my own and, within two
months, I could cough or sneeze or laugh without
any concern. I even stopped putting tissues in my
panties as a precaution. It's not necessary anymore.*

Or maybe you reacted like this man from Maine:

*Reading about the importance of muscle tone was
of enormous help to us. After Kim had our third*

child, intercourse began to be much less enjoyable for me. Kim was simply too large and soft. I felt constrained about saying anything to her. It didn't seem fair to complain about something that had happened as a result of her bearing our children, particularly since there wasn't anything to do about it. After hearing about your work, I gathered the courage to mention to Kim that it might be helpful if she did some of those Kegel exercises. We even practiced sometimes with me inside of her. And, oh, what a difference that has made to both of us. It turns out that Kim wasn't enjoying our sex as much either, and now we're having a great time again.

Or maybe, like this man of seventy and his sixty-five-year-old wife, you also acted on this new information:

In the past few years, it has been more difficult for Mary to reach orgasm through intercourse, something that was never a problem in the earlier years of our marriage. After learning about the two paths to orgasm, we decided to try using clitoral stimulation while having intercourse. It was a real help to Mary. If we had continued to believe in intercourse to the exclusion of clitoral stimulation, we would never have gotten the courage to explore in that way.

One couple wrote that they decided, for the first time in their lives, to buy a vibrator in order to explore the blended orgasms about which the Singers wrote:

> *We looked over the mail order catalogue and ordered a vibrator so that we could stimulate my clitoris vigorously at the same time Jim was thrusting. We don't really need this, but it is a delightful variation on our more conventional lovemaking.*

A self-proclaimed Don Juan complained that our research had cost him his racer's edge:

> *For twenty-five years, I've led an active social and sexual life because I went to the effort of discovering as much about male and female plumbing as I could with the sole purpose of becoming sexually adept. Your discovery and its publicity has cost me a well kept and very valuable trade secret.*

Little does he realize that he has not been, nor will he ever be, the sole possessor of "the secret." For there are many people out there like this older couple, who wrote:

> *My God, are you people just finding out about that Gräfenberg deal? My wife and I have been married fifty-one years and we found that particular place less than six months after first intercourse. We called it "Rabbit Nose." And still do. I am seventy-six and she is sixty-nine. Due to various circumstances we did not reach that climax on every occasion, but did at least 90 percent of the time.*

Some people, like the man who wrote the following letter, felt the need to caution us about the possible negative effects of our findings: "Unfortunately, it isn't possible to control how the information you develop will be perceived or used. This new knowledge should not add more pressure to the strained personal situations many of us experience sexually." And he is quite right. Not everyone was overjoyed with the "news." Only two letters expressed outrage, believing that such information should be confined "to doctors' offices, private meetings, and closed-circuit TV," but several people, like this thirty-two-year-old woman from Pennsylvania, wrote that they did feel new pressures now:

> *My husband used to ask whenever we made love, "Did you come, did you come?" I didn't like that very much. It seemed to me that he should know without asking, and it also felt like a demand. Now guess what he says? "Did you spurt, did you spurt?" Sometimes I feel like hitting him . . . only I don't. He should be able to tell that! And anyway I don't ejaculate and never have. It was bad enough being watched over about having a climax. Now I'm supposed to ejaculate.*

Here's a comment from a Native American woman living in South Dakota who believes that her former equilibrium has been disturbed:

> *Now my husband insists that every woman has a G spot, and last night he spent an hour trying to get me to find mine. I have always enjoyed clitoral stimulation, and until we learned about your work, Raymond was perfectly content with our sex life. Now he's so eager to explore new ways that we're fighting all the time.*

Or consider this protest from a man of twenty-five:

> *Since my wife learned about the G spot and female
> ejaculation, she refuses to allow me to play with her
> clitoris either with my finger or my tongue. She
> always used to enjoy that. But now she insists that
> we have intercourse without much foreplay (which
> I like a lot), and she berates me for being a bad lover
> because I don't help her to ejaculate. I haven't got
> the world's greatest staying power, but I don't shoot
> off that quickly either. Why did you have to spoil our
> fun?*

It would be comforting to conclude that these couples are
the exception, not the rule, that their responses reflect unusual
hostility or ways of communicating that are rare. Although we
received many fewer responses of this nature, the comments,
in our opinion, do reflect a way of thinking that is unfortunately quite widespread.

One source of pressure derives from the need to conform.
We live in a culture that pays lip-service to the virtues of individuality and uniqueness, exhorting people to "do their own
thing," to be original and creative, to be themselves. Yet every
group and segment of society has unspoken rules. Even those
rebellious, sexually free, nonconforming hippies of the not-so-
distant past had a code of their own. In some places we are
made to feel out of place if we are unfashionably dressed, in
others if we are too fashionable. Some people applaud regular
church attendance, others mock it. Liberated mothers encourage their boys to play with dolls while traditional mothers are
horrified if their sons prefer poetry to baseball. There are com-
munities where being homosexual is akin to being criminal,
and others where being gay is considered beautiful. Just try

being the resident Democrat in a Republican community, or vice versa. The pressure to conform is all around us.

This book is filled with examples of men and women who felt uncomfortable because their sexual experiences were different from what they thought they "ought" to be. A few discussed their presumed abnormalities with other people, but some, like this man from Alaska, gave up and decided to say nothing further:

> *I was talking with my brother about sex. He was talking about what would make his wife come (sorry about that word, but it was the word he used). I said, "Women don't do that!" He said, "Yes, they do too." I said, "You're nuts," and that was all that was ever said about it. But over the years, every so often, when having intercourse with my wife, I would be aware of a shooting stream of fluid banging up against the sides of my penis. It felt like a stream of water from a water gun. It came in spurts. There would be anywhere from three to six spurts. I asked her the first time it happened if she had had some sort of ejaculation. She said, No, that she had not noticed anything like that. I said, "You mean you did not feel anything spurt out of you?" She said, "No, it must be your imagination." So from then on I just did not say anything. I noticed it and thought and studied my mind on it, but I would just keep quiet about it, as I figured I would just get the same answer from her.*

Like thousands of others who wrote to say that they had never discussed their sex lives with anyone before, this man now wanted to share his private experiences in the hope of helping others who may have been feeling similarly confused about themselves or their partners.

> *Now I know why my ex-wife preferred certain positions or movements during coitus. (Sex was one of the successful aspects of our marriage.) I hope I don't offend by being too graphic, but one of her favorite positions was with me supine in a reclining rocking lounge chair. She would lie atop me or straddle me. The rocker-recliner added to our motions greatly. We never told anyone about this.*

One concern we have is that people may use the new information to spoil the pleasure they already enjoy. Instead of enriching their lives, knowledge about the G spot and female ejaculation could focus the attention of some readers on what they mistakenly assume to be the "best" and thus interfere with the good that already exists.

We don't want to create new pressures for women or men. Sex is for pleasure, and when it becomes goal-oriented, the pleasure is often diminished. The facts we have presented indicate that there are many dimensions to the way people experience sexual climax and orgasm. We want women who ejaculate, for example, to know that it is a natural response and that it's okay to enjoy it. This knowledge should be available, without being converted into pressure to conform. We want women who do not ejaculate to feel all right about that, too, to enjoy whatever kind of pleasure they experience and not strive for ejaculation or worry that they or their partners may be missing something essential.

Sexuality is a part of life, everyone's life. We are born sexual creatures and remain so all our days. But it is our choice how we express it. Sexuality is a much broader subject than genital sex. It involves touching, holding, and many other activities. Being held by someone can, on occasion, be completely fulfilling, as can touching someone's hand. There are people who choose never to experience a sexual relationship that involves genital contact with another person. Climax or orgasm is not the inevitable goal. Many adults, imagining that it is expected of them, intrude genital sex into relationships where it does not belong at all, thus limiting an otherwise rich association. Some of us miss out on many warm relationships because we are afraid the sensual expression of friendship must, of necessity, be consummated with genital sex. Just because most men and women are interested in genital sex, it would be an error to insist that all are or should be. Some therapists believe that people who do not seek a genital sexual partnership, or even a snuggling partnership with anyone, avoid such contact because of fear and deep hurts that were inflicted on them early in infancy and childhood. Nevertheless, there are celibates who are quite comfortable with their decision to remain genitally sexually inactive. Being made to feel that this choice is wrong, second-best, or a mark of inferiority will certainly not help anyone who has chosen to live this way to feel better about life. Those who do not intentionally or happily choose genital sexual isolation but nonetheless live that way because they cannot help themselves may find that change is possible if they wish to attempt it. In such situations, it is often useful to seek help from a qualified professional. (See Appendix B.)

Even in a relationship where genital sex is appropriate and desired by both parties, orgasm may still not be the goal. As one woman put it: "The whole question of whether I do/did or don't/didn't reach a climax and/or orgasm, and what's the difference, made me miserable for years and contributed to and/or was caused by extreme feelings of inadequacy. I finally quit caring."

She did not say what made it possible for her to quit caring, but similar sentiments are echoed in *Sex, the Facts, the Acts and Your Feelings*, a recent book by Michael Carrera, Ed.D.

Q: When I have an orgasm it feels good and I enjoy it, but it certainly doesn't feel anything like those I read about in magazines and books. Should I seek some professional help?

A: No. Most literature describing orgasm sets up unrealistic standards and expectations. We get images of unbelievably explosive orgasms, measure our own experiences against them, and conclude that ours are nowhere near the "ideal."

The important thing to remember about *your* sex life is that it should be fulfilling for *you* and *your partner*. Your sexual feelings are unique and so are your partner's. The way you respond to each other is unique too. Descriptions of orgasms you read may well be idealized, and even if they are truthful, they are someone else's experience, which can never be the same as your own. Trying to match your feelings with accounts of other people's can only interfere with your enjoyment.[1]

Sexual activity should be a pleasurable experience and not a performance requiring some specified outcome. Pleasure, enjoyment, and the path of mutual exploration and sharing are more important than any end result. The subject of sex reaches deep into our most elemental feelings and touches us in the most sensitive areas of our being. New information about it must not add pressure.

When she was a child, Alice Ladas recalls visiting a well-furnished home with conspicuously bare walls. Overcome by curiosity, she asked why there were no pictures in the house. "Because," came the reply, "unless we can hang a Rembrandt or a Rubens, we prefer to hang nothing at all." This sort of struggle to have the best (whatever that may be) or to be the best can be the enemy of the good. Her friend's parents insisted on the best or nothing—so they lived in a barren house.

Many folktales, fairy tales, and historical myths remind us of the pitfalls that lie in the path of pursuing the best, whether from motives of greed or competition. Consider the story of the fisherman and his malcontent wife. The old man catches a magic fish who pleads to be released and, in return, promises to grant three wishes to the elderly pair. Their first wish, for a small cottage, is granted. But the old woman wants something better and so she asks for a mansion. That wish too is fulfilled, but the wife then longs for a palace. When she finds herself in a place less grand than her dreams had pictured, she insists that her husband return a fourth time with the request for a grander palace. Angered by the woman's insatiability, the fish sends the couple back to the mud hut where they were living at the start.

We all have friends who, in their obsessive pursuit of perfection, develop ulcers, colitis, constipation, and other gastrointestinal disorders. Anorexia nervosa, that mysterious and intractable disease that is afflicting more and more women today, is also associated with striving to be the "best" (i.e. the thinnest).

Writers, lecturers, and actors who portray the best in glowing terms unintentionally transmit to their audiences the tacit messages that their lives are far from ideal. Psychologists and marital and family therapists well know how many divorces result from focusing on what is lacking in a relationship when compared to some ideal. Rather than building on the good that already exists, partners separate and search for the "best" in someone new, often with the same results.

Sex in any form is an exciting topic, and most people pay attention to it, even when it is not the thing itself but only words or pictures describing it. As a culture we have gone from the tyranny of Victorianism, to the tyranny of the clitoral-vaginal transfer theory, to the tyranny of the central role of the clitoris, to the tyranny of having to have an orgasm, and even perhaps to the tyranny of having to be sexually active. Because we have reached a new synthesis with regard to certain aspects of sexuality, let's not establish another tyranny involving the G spot, female ejaculation, multiple orgasm, or the male prostate. Let's keep in mind that we are all unique, all different from one another and from ourselves at different periods in our lives. No two of us experience life in exactly the same way, although there are vast areas of similarity.

We don't even know, for example, whether all women are capable of having an orgasm. Many women, but not all, say they have experienced some type of climax. Many women who sought professional help have found that they were able to reach climax for the first time, or that they were able to achieve a deeper, orgasmic response—but again, some women do not experience any change at all. Although some sex researchers have presumed that inability to reach orgasm is abnormal and have even labeled women who enjoy their sexuality but do not have an orgasm as inadequate, we have evidence from women themselves that they do not believe this is so. Other well respected sex researchers support them in that view. Helen Singer Kaplan,[2] among others, believes that sexual responsiveness that does not include orgasm may be normal for a sizable group of women.

The subject of satisfaction is also relevant. Many women report full satisfaction with their sex lives and yet they never experience orgasm. Seymour Fisher, Ph.D., points out that "there is no indication that the capacity to attain consistent orgasm provides an incentive for a woman to seek a high frequency of intercourse."[3] But greater *satisfaction* does appear to provide just such an incentive. This conclusion is reported by another sex researcher in conjunction with the finding that emotional closeness with a partner is considered the most enjoyable aspect of sex and more important than consistency of orgasmic response.[4]

A male patient recently asked:

> *You mean I shouldn't get angry with Jennifer if she doesn't have an orgasm? I don't want her to have sex just as an accommodation to me, but when she doesn't come, I think that's what she's doing.*

To which Jennifer replied:

> *That's nonsense. Sometimes I come, sometimes I don't. It depends on a lot of things. But I can tell you this, there are times when I don't have a climax but I feel wonderfully close to you. And there are other times when I have an orgasm, but I don't feel so good with you. And I much prefer the first to the latter. So get off my back about coming. An orgasm isn't something you can deliver on command. Stop making the whole issue so important.*

A forty-two-year-old woman reported, "Some of the most ecstatic experiences in my life have *not* culminated in orgasm."

Sexual expression is not an Olympic contest, with gold, silver, and bronze medals for each event. On the contrary, given correct information and enough support so that people can find their own particular and personal way to enjoyment and satisfaction, everybody can win.

One woman, aged twenty-five, said:

> *I've reached a climax through Mark stroking my clitoris, but much more satisfying for me is that delicious melting sensation (which I equate with love) that we experience when he is inside of me. It's very rare that I experience orgasm under these circumstances but I would choose this experience any day over the "orgasm" I experience the other way.*

The *Hite Report* is full of contradictory evidence of how women feel about orgasm: "Whoever said orgasm wasn't important for a woman was undoubtedly a man" is followed by "Women are now under great pressure to perform by having orgasms, especially during intercourse." A few women, Shere Hite observed, react strongly against this pressure to perform, but there is also a social pressure that says that a woman who has an orgasm is more of a woman, a "real" woman. Yet other women came to the conclusion that orgasm during sex was not important.[5]

It is easy to find women who subscribe to any and all of these views, even to find one woman who subscribes to all of them simultaneously. Greta, forty-eight and married for the second time, said:

> *I feel badly, and so does John, when I don't have an orgasm for several weeks. It seems to me that I am*

> *less than a whole woman, and yet I know in my*
> *head that isn't true. I wonder why we're built so*
> *that men almost always and easily reach a climax in*
> *intercourse, while for women it's not such a certain*
> *thing.*

Some theorists suspect this is a culturally induced phenomenon, although we don't yet have the data from all cultures to fully substantiate such a view. What we do know is that many women today report being multiply orgasmic, while some men are choosing to practice a form of sex where intercourse, by choice, does not always culminate in ejaculation, and which sometimes allows them to be multiply orgasmic as well. A few men have reported that the pleasure of this experience is even greater than that of intercourse culminating in ejaculation.[6]

Psychiatrist Avodah Offit, M.D., in her book *The Sexual Self* reminds us, "We can tell who we are and what we believe by observing how we act, think, dream and feel sexually. We express our most fundamental natures through our sexual choices."[7] The remainder of her book describes in detail the problems and difficulties which beset various personality types. As with many handbooks of psychiatric diagnosis, the emphasis is on the negative. Since most of us fall into one or another of the categories described, and the problems not the assets of each type are emphasized, the final picture appears to be one of a world in which nobody can win, and no one experiences true pleasure, satisfaction, or joy, except perhaps fleetingly. If that is true, how can we explain the thousands of letters from satisfied couples who have been privately and quietly enjoying and exploring their sexual potential?

It depends on what kind of glasses the observer is wearing. Whatever the fundamental truth about life may be, viewing it as an inevitable vale of tears does not encourage laughter and joy. Accentuating the positive may be just as unrealistic, but that attitude does help to relax the autonomic nervous system, the branch that works without conscious control and allows us to function with a bit more ease, so that pleasure may be enhanced.

Whatever the truth is about women and orgasm—that all women have the potential for all kinds, that some women have the potential for one type and some for another, that women are frustrated sexually if they fail to reach a climax, or that some are quite satisfied and even ecstatic without it—one thing is certainly true: pressure to achieve something that involves the autonomic nervous system often has the opposite effect. *No one reaches orgasm by an act of will*. Because of variations in endocrine balance, brain chemistry, and exposure to different life experiences, there is no one uniform pattern of sexual response.

Orgasm, like breast-feeding, depends upon many factors that the body will handle on its own when not interfered with. Just as the "let down" reflex, essential to breast-feeding, will not occur in the presence of fear (peace of mind must also be present—the milk may be there, but the flow will only begin when it is not blocked by constriction of muscles and nerves), enjoyment of genital sexual pleasure is not consistent with a mental set that demands high standards of performance. It occurs much more easily and naturally when one lets the sensory apparatus take over without interference. This does not negate the value of education, for information and support are also important to healthy sexual response. But the thought of having to perform, having to be the "best," is antithetical to pleasurable sexual response.

The famous tenor Luciano Pavarotti tells the story that when he was twenty-six he was so little in demand as a singer that he gave a series of recitals without charge. The next to the last recital "was a disaster. I sounded like a baritone who was being strangled," and resolved to give up singing when the series was finished. But having given up the struggle, he sang so magnificently at his final concert that his singing career was launched.[8]

The sensate focus exercises that Masters and Johnson developed to help couples overcome certain sexual difficulties encourage men and women to focus on the process rather than on the end result. Essentially, couples are instructed to take turns touching each other, first in areas that are not highly erotic and later in areas that are. At first the recipient is just to experience the sensation and, later, feedback to the partner is encouraged. This gives couples the chance to let each other know, without the onus of appearing critical, what they do not like and just what it is that gives them pleasure. The experiences are not supposed to culminate in intercourse for a certain period of time. The trick, as every Zen master knows, is that by focusing on the process, the desired end result often occurs without any conscious thought or effort. As Timothy Gallwey explained in *The Inner Game of Tennis*:

> The player of the inner game comes to value the art of relaxed concentration above all other skills; he discovers a true basis for self-confidence; and he learns that the secret to winning any game lies in not trying too hard. He aims at the kind of spontaneous performance which occurs only when the mind is calm and seems at one with the body . . . There is a far more natural and effective process for learning and doing almost anything than most of us realize. It is similar to the process we all used, but soon forgot, as we learned to walk and talk. It uses the so-called uncon-

scious mind more than the deliberate "self-con-
scious" mind, the spinal and mid-brain areas of the
nervous system more than the cerebral cortex. This
process doesn't have to be learned; we already know
it. All that is needed is to *unlearn* those habits which
interfere with it and then to just *let it happen.*[9]

What is the "best" anyway? Best is an illusion, an absolute,
and absolutes are not attainable. An eminent art dealer told us
about having to rescue canvases from an equally eminent
painter who has trouble completing paintings because he keeps
working them over and over again trying to attain perfection.
The art dealer had this to say about "best":

> *The word implies perfection, which is insidious,
> decadent, and boring. "Best" is a value judgment,
> but you have to ask from what point of view it is
> being judged.*
>
> *The best is idealistic. The good is safe ground.
> Best is treacherous. It is better to enjoy the good
> than to fail at the best. Striving for the best may be
> okay but attaining the best is a danger point. When
> you reach the goal and stop striving, life becomes a
> vacuum. The best denies process. One must never
> arrive or the spark of life is dampened.*

The North Star is a guide not a goal. If the earth moved once
for the hero and heroine of Hemingway's *For Whom the Bell
Tolls*, that does not mean it must move each time a loving couple has intercourse. To create a standard and then make it into
a demand is a sure formula for creating unhappiness. It is nice
when the earth moves, but it is not something to expect or to
demand. Indeed, the very expectation may make it impossible.

Yet some things can be improved. Working toward progress on a gradient scale is possible and realistic. Good yoga teachers advise their pupils to compare themselves only with themselves, and to work at their own self-selected pace. Satisfied people tend to set moderate, step-by-step goals that have a high possibility of being achieved. Dissatisfied people often have grandiose goals, "best" goals if you will, which they are unlikely to achieve and which leave them disconsolate or depressed when they fail to reach them.

The best is, of course, the enemy of the good in another sense. The winner of a contest is the best, and he is, in some sense, the enemy of the many good contenders who didn't or maybe never will win. But that is a rather special situation. The Kennedy children, especially the boys, were raised to be the "best," and several of them paid dearly for their ambitions.

Where competition is not the issue, as in sex, the risk of pursuing the best is very likely not worth it, for the pursuit itself may deflect the goal. Often the secret of success, at some point, lies in not trying. Not striving is the key to biofeedback relaxation training, it is the key to meditation, it is the key to the martial arts. Hans Selye, M.D., father of stress research, advises us to "admit that there is no perfection . . ."

The error is not in making judgments. We all do that. It is in making judgments based on unrealistic or obsessively competitive standards. For example, if you happen to be a runner who runs an eight-minute mile, you might decide to try to run a seven-and-a-half-minute mile, and that would probably be a sensible goal. But if instead you decide to try to win the Boston Marathon, you are setting an unrealistic standard and are bound to be disappointed, unless you have the proper body structure and talent, and are willing to undergo the necessary physical training. Applying the same logic to sex by attempting to become a multiply orgasmic ejaculator overnight—when you may not be physically or mentally equipped—will also create misery.

Then there is the "grass is always greener" syndrome. Are things better for my next-door neighbor, my best friend, or my spouse, than for me? The fallacy in this sort of thinking is that you often have no idea what the other person is actually experiencing. In the case of the next-door neighbor, perhaps he or she has the best marriage, the most talented children, and the best orgasms. But you don't know, and you may be striving for something inferior to what you already have. Even if the "grass is really greener," you won't help yourself by making comparisons.

Although some people look upon sex as a competitive activity, it is more realistic to view it as one that everyone can enjoy and participate in. Don't assume that others are getting all the goodies. You can read this book and say to yourself, "I should be experiencing more and better ejaculations, more and better orgasms like everyone else," or you can read this book and conclude that there are new areas of experience worth exploring. You may have learned some things you did not know before, and you may decide to see if those things are within the range of possibility for your relationships and your body. Deciding to have "the ultimate sexual experience" will likely lead to disappointment and may itself prevent the desired experience from occurring.

Psychologists, psychiatrists, and clinicians tell us that basic character defines the parameters of our sexual behavior, and that character is not easy to change. "We develop personality characteristics largely in response to the way our parents treated us," said Offit.[10] It goes without saying that none of us can change what our parents did to us in the past, although we can change our view of what they did and our reactions to it.

But therapists are constantly reminding us that even that is extremely difficult to do.

It is our belief, nevertheless, that quite a few people will be able to improve their lives substantially using the knowledge in this book. Letters from all over the country confirm that view. They tell us that "now that I know some women prefer vaginal to clitoral stimulation, I don't have to worry that there is something wrong with me"; "now that I know that ejaculation is normal for many women, I no longer feel 'weird'"; "now that I know that muscle tone is an important factor in my response, I am working to strengthen my PC muscle, and I no longer feel helpless or ashamed about my lack of responsiveness"; "now that I know that many men prefer prostatic to penile stimulation, I am no longer afraid to ask for this from my female partner," and much more.

Most people never have and never will see therapists or clinicians. They may lack the problems, the motivation, the opportunity, or the money, but still may want to improve, change, or enhance their sexual lives. Perhaps you reach a climax or an orgasm through clitoral stimulation but you would like to experiment and see whether vaginal responsiveness is possible for you. You may want to try a different position, learn to breathe more freely, or move your pelvis. Perhaps your internal or external pelvic muscles are chronically contracted and you want to see whether you can change that. On the other hand, maybe you and your partner are content with your clitoral response.

There are also people who have never had an orgasm of any kind (as it has been described in this book), but who are content with their sexual lives, satisfied with their partners, and not interested in experimenting further. That's fine too.

Maybe you are one of those women who become extremely

excited by sexual contact, and feel that you are always on the edge of coming and can never get over the hump. If so, the information in this book may assist you in getting some constructive help.

All the talk and excitement about sexuality that has bombarded us in the past decades has not only been liberating, it has, in many instances, been coercive, not only to young people who may feel that an active sex life is a must or the "in" thing, but also to older people who believe that something must be wrong with them if they are no longer sexually active.

We have been speaking mostly about women, but similar statements can be made about men. Like women, some men want and need a great deal of sexual activity. Some men have orgasms that involve their entire body and others have local genital climaxes. Some want to learn to be multiply orgasmic. Others want to explore the sexual sensations generated by stimulation of their prostate gland. Others need to be cuddled or held. But for many men, these things are simply irrelevant and unimportant. There is no *one* best way. There are *many* good and satisfying life-styles.

One thing is certain. We are creatures of variety in sexual matters, as in all other areas. Kinsey was a pioneer in telling us about who does what with whom. Is one way better than another? Who can judge for anyone else? Although the life-style each of us chooses is related to our biological heritage, our basic character structure, and our cultural background, as long as the sexual style we choose is personally satisfying and socially not harmful to another human being or to ourselves, there is no need to question it, evaluate it, or place it in some position on a scale of better to worse.

It is likely that many women and men who read this book will want to explore the possibilities of orgasmic response through stimulation of the G spot, will want to explore the possibility of female ejaculation, will want to know more about their own pelvic muscle tone or the prostate gland. Many will want to discover if they can add to their repertoire of sexual responses for the sake of variety and pleasure. Make the most of the information. Let it support you, inform you, guide you. Don't let it tyrannize you or tell you what you ought to feel, be, or do.

As long as you recognize that "the best is the enemy of the good," *the good can become the best* at any moment in time, because *it is* what you experience.

APPENDIXES

Appendix A

Pubococcygeus Muscle Training Aids

The original Kegel Perineometer operated by air pressure and measured the physical displacement of the vaginal walls under the influence of the pubococcygeus muscles that surround them. Vaginal myography, in contrast, directly measures the electrical activity of the pubococcygeus muscle itself.

"EMG" is short for "electro-myographic" biofeedback, which has developed as a form of therapy only during the past decade. EMG sensors, when placed over a muscle, detect the minute electrical charges that take place when muscle fibers are activated by the nerves. The accumulated total of these tiny charges, measured in microvolts, provides an accurate measure of the total amount of muscle activity.

EMG is now widely used in the rehabilitation of the muscles of stroke and paralysis victims, but in the past researchers had difficulty fastening or securing the traditional one-inch-diameter sensors to the vaginal wall. The vaginal myograph probe, which is sold under the trade-name "Electronic Perineometer," is one solution that many therapists have found convenient for office and home use. Information about the Electronic Perineometer is available from Health Technology, Inc. (50 Lawn Avenue, Portland, Maine 04103). Health Technology also sponsors a training program in the techniques of vaginal myography that is offered for professionals in various cities each year.

The Electronic Perineometer may be used with any of the commercially available EMG biofeedback instruments. Recently, two new products expressly designed to be used with the Electronic Perineometer in vaginal muscle evaluation and training as described in this book have been introduced. The Clinical Perineometer is a desktop instrument designed to provide a complete diagnostic evaluation of PC muscle strength, tension, and control. It includes a strip chart recorder (similar to an EKG), which permits detailed examination of the patterns of muscle contraction. A light bar and audible tone provide biofeedback for training purposes. The Personal Perineometer is a hand-held patient take-home unit designed to be used during the first few weeks of PC muscle training. It includes a light bar and tone for biofeedback. The Electronic Perineometer sensor is included with both instruments, also available from Health Technology.

Kegel recommended that a "resistive device" always be used as a part of his muscle training program when undertaken for medical reasons, or in cases of severe muscle weakness or atrophy. A new device has been introduced that is made of firm latex and fits comfortably in the vagina during exercise. Called the Femtone Isometric Vaginal Exerciser, it is available from J. & L. Feminine Research Center (2509 North Campbell Avenue, Suite 196-G1, Tucson, Arizona 85719).

Although the Femtone was designed expressly for women training their PC muscles, equally good results can be obtained using a latex rubber "dildo," or artificial penis. These are commonly sold in shops that carry sexual aids. People who do not wish to purchase them over the counter might find it more convenient to shop by mail. There are several reliable mail-order houses, including Eve's Garden (119 West 57th Street, New York, New York 10019), Adam and Eve (P.O. Box 800, Carrboro, North Carolina 27510), Good Vibrations (3416 22nd Street, San Francisco, California 94110), and The Xandra Collection (P.O. Box 31039, San Francisco, California 94131).

A new form of vaginal exerciser made of solid brass is available from The Institute for Sexual Awareness (P.O. Drawer 828, Upper Montclair, New Jersey 07043). A variety of other devices have been marketed in recent years, including modern "ben-wa-balls," and various air-pressure or fluid-filled perineometers. Many of them might be useful to women seeking to improve their PC muscles, but we have not systematically evaluated them.

Two devices for electro-stimulation of the PC muscle, the Vagitone and the Vagette #76, are both currently available through the mail-order houses listed above.

"Electronic Perioneometer" (patents pending) is a trademark of Health Technology, Inc. "Clinical Perioneometer" and "Personal Perioneometer" are trademarks of Farrall Instruments, Inc. "Femtone Isometric Vaginal Exerciser" is a registered trademark of J. & L. Feminine Research Center. The Vagette #76 is a registered trademark of Myodynamics, Inc.

Appendix B

National Referral Sources for Therapy

The following organizations can provide you with specific information or guide you to a qualified therapist:

American Association of Marriage and Family Therapists, 924 West Ninth Street, Upland, California 91786

American Association of Sex Educators, Counselors and Therapists, 600 Maryland Avenue, S.W., Washington, D.C. 20024

The American College of Sexologists, 1523 Franklin Street, San Francisco, California 94109

The Association of Sexologists, 1537 Franklin Street, San Francisco, California 94109

Biofeedback Certification Institute of America, 4301 Owens Street, Wheat Ridge, Colorado 80033

International Institute for Bioenergetic Analysis, 144 East 36th Street, New York, New York 10016

Sex Information and Education Council of the United States, 84 Fifth Avenue, Suite 407, New York, New York 10011

The Society for the Scientific Study of Sex, Inc., P.O. Box 29795, Philadelphia, Pennsylvania 19117

The Society for Sex Therapy and Research, c/o Oliver Bjoiksten, M.D., Medical University of South Carolina, Department of Psychiatry, 171 Ashley Avenue, Charleston, South Carolina 29425

Additional suggestions may be obtained from your state medical society, state psychological society, or state biofeedback society, which are usually listed in the telephone directory.

Appendix C

Abstract, Tables, and Conclusions
From *Women and Bioenergetic Analysis*
by Alice Kahn Ladas and Harold Ladas

Sexual Beliefs, experiences, and practices of 134 Women (members of the Institute for Bioenergetic Analysis—a neo-Freudian body-oriented psychotherapy).

Abstract

A questionnaire was mailed to 198 women, the total female membership in 1977 of The Institute for Bioenergetic Analysis, a neo-Freudian body-oriented psychotherapy training organization. Sixty-eight percent (134) returned valid replies. The areas covered by the questionnaire included the effects on themselves and patients of the therapy, an assessment of their views of bioenergetic theory, and their sexual beliefs, experiences, and practices. This paper focuses primarily on heterosexual experiences and beliefs.

As predicted, 81 percent of the respondents reported improvement in their sexual life following therapy. Unexpectedly, up to 87 percent of the respondents disagreed with one or more of the theories of Alexander Lowen, M.D., founder of Bioenergetic Analysis, as they apply

TABLE 1

Effect of Bioenergetic Analysis on Women in the Study (N = 134)

Outcome	Relative percent finding it helpful	Adjusted percent finding it helpful**
Self assertion	89	94
Breathing	89	94
Self esteem	86	93
Capacity to experience pleasure	86	92
Capacity to love	83	89
Physical health	79	74
Ability to cope with depression	79	84
Diminished chronic muscle tension	77	83
Energy level	77	83
Unification of sexual and tender feelings in relationship	68	73
Involuntary movement in orgasm	63	67
Finding a partner	45	49
Sleep problems	33	38
Menopause*	17	18
Menstruation	16	17
Interaction with infants*	7	7
Coping with unwanted habits, e.g.		
Overeating	23	30
Smoking	12	17
Enjoyment in breast-feeding*	5	6
Chosen manner of infant feeding*	5	6

*Most subjects responded "Not Applicable."
**Adjusted by subtracting respondents who did not answer.

to female sexuality. Although 73 percent of the respondents reported experiencing vaginal orgasm, 87 percent felt, nonetheless, that the clitoris is important and should not be ignored.

TABLE 2

Effect of Bioenergetic Analysis on Sexual Responses

Outcome	Before B.A.		After B.A.		Percent Change
	Yes	No	Yes	No	
Has your experience of sexual climax changed since bioenergetic analysis?			81	19	81
If yes, how:					
More generalized body experience			59		
Breathe more deeply			62		
Pelvis moves more freely			54		
Pelvis moves more involuntarily			43		
Fantasize less			23		
Experience more sweet feelings			45		
Feeling centered more deeply in the vagina			41		
Have you experienced orgasm (as contrasted to sexual climax)?	51	49	80	20	29
Have you experienced turning in of energy along walls and deep in your vagina?	44	56	66	34	22
Have you experienced streamings?	36	64	76	24	40

Note: Percent adjusted by eliminating missing cases on a given item.

TABLE 3

Women Consider the Role of the Clitoris

	Before B.A.		After B.A.	
Outcome	Yes	No	Yes	No
Have you experienced a sexual climax through intercourse without any special clitoral stimulation?	60	40	73	27
Through intercourse with clitoral stimulation by partner?	78	22	81	19
Through intercourse with clitoral stimulation by yourself?	42	58	51	49
Through clitoral stimulation, no intercourse?	83	17	87	13

Note: Percent adjusted by eliminating missing cases on a given item.

TABLE 4

Agreement with Bioenergetic Analytic Theory*

Theoretical statement	Strongly Disagree	Disagree	No Opinion	Agree	Strongly Agree	Total
"Man is woman's bridge to the outside world."	62	24	4.5	3.0	1.5	86**
Stimulation of the clitoris (directly or indirectly) in intercourse is not important for the mature woman.	51	36	2.4	10.3	5.3	87**
"The clitoral orgasm is felt on the surface of the vagina like a trickle of	43	35	5	10.0	1.5	78**

Table 4 (cont'd)

Theoretical statement	Strongly Disagree	Disagree	No Opinion	Agree	Strongly Agree	Total
sweet pleasure. There is no satisfying release."						
"Tactile stimulation in itself is not a causative factor in erotic arousal."	17	53	4	17.0	2.0	70°°
It is often helpful if a man can postpone his climax until a woman approaches hers.	6	6	10	58.0	19.0	77°°°
Many women require direct or indirect clitoral stimulation in order to reach a sexual climax.	2	1	3	62.0	26.0	88°°°
For the well-being of both, men would do well to help their women get direct or indirect clitoral stimulation when desired.	—	2	4	56.0	30.0	86°°°

Note: Percent adjusted by eliminating missing cases on a given item.
° As formulated by Alexander Lowen in *Love and Orgasm*.
°° Total of strongly disagree plus disagree
°°°Total of strongly agree plus agree.

Conclusion

Women in bioenergetic analysis are clearly not true believers, which gives additional credence to the positive findings of the study. Respondents certainly believe that they and their clients have benefitted from bioenergetic analysis therapy although they disagree with some items of theory. Despite this, and in spite of the fact that one of the main benefits women report from bioenergetic analysis is the increased capacity to assert themselves (89 percent), they did not find it easy to express these disagreements either verbally at meetings or in writing. Perhaps this is partially a political problem.

Fundamentally, the problems that occur in the Institute for Bioenergetic Analysis and its local societies are a reflection of the kind of difficulties that women encounter in our society generally. This is a period when all of us are rethinking our sexual roles. Our thinking is heavily influenced by the ideas with which we live and also our actions and our perceptions are influenced by these ideas. It will take time before we begin to change them and, as a result, to perceive and act differently. One way to start that process is to speak with each other, listen to each other, and begin a dialogue. Perhaps this study will facilitate that process.

A copy of this twenty-seven-page monograph can be obtained from the Connecticut Society for Bioenergetic Analysis, 2804 Whitney Avenue, Hamden, Connecticut 06518, for $3.00, which includes postage and handling.

Questionnaire on Female Sexuality: Work in Progress (Processed to Date N = 131) Alice K. Ladas

This questionnaire is exploratory and intended to provide information about what professionals believe. It is not intended at this point to provide measures of central tendency or variation in the professional population. Numbers in bold face are percentages unless otherwise indicated. When percentages don't add up to 100 a few respondents had created additional categories.

Instructions: If you are a woman, answer all the questions yourself. Some questions refer to a partner. If you are a man, answer those questions for your female partner.

Check one answer for each statement unless otherwise indicated.

Number of respondents who answered item

My anatomical sex is:
1. **19** male   2. **81** female   131

My sexual preference is:
1. **95** heterosexual   2. **2** homosexual
3. **4** bisexual   130

If you make a distinction between climax and orgasm, what do you regard as some of the differences? (Check one or the other column.)

Climax		*Orgasm*	
12	Breathing is deeper	87	60
10	The heart is more involved	90	61
3	Involuntary contractions extend over the entire body	92	63
10	Involuntary sounds occur	80	59
43	Involuntary contractions occur primarily in the pelvic area	50	54
14	Other—describe	57	7

Are there any sensory nerve endings in the vagina?
1. **56** yes   2. **16** no   3. **28** don't know   127

Is there a particularly sensitive place (or places) inside your vagina? (Check any that apply.)
1. **78** yes   2. **12** no   3. **10** don't know   101
1. **31** one   2. **40** two   3. **29** more than two   55

If there is a specially sensitive spot in your partner's vagina, does it get stimulated during intercourse?
1. **71** yes   2. **14** no   3. **14** sometimes   21

If there is a specially sensitive spot in your vagina, does it get stimulated during intercourse?
1. **46** yes   2. **6** no   3. **47** sometimes   93

Number of
respondents
who answered
item

What positions best stimulate that spot? (Check any that apply.)°

67 front entry   29 rear entry—woman on stomach

24 woman on knees   19 rear entry—woman on side

5 anal entry   10 other—describe

If there is a specially sensitive spot in your vagina, can it be stimulated manually?

1. 58 yes   2. 22 no   3. 20 don't know   95

Is there such a thing as female ejaculation?

1. 32 yes   2. 28 no   3. 39 don't know   127

Do you have personal experience with female ejaculation?

1. 32 yes   2. 73 no   111

If female, do you ejaculate?

1. 12 yes   2. 37 no   3. 39 not sure

4. 12 sometimes   98

Have you ever been afraid of urinating when sexually aroused?

1. 42 yes   2. 57 no   125

Has your partner ever been afraid of urinating when sexually aroused?

1. 16 yes   2. 81 no   81

Have you ever thought you urinated when having a sexual climax?

1. 31 yes   2. 69 no   127

Have you ever thought your partner urinated while having a sexual climax?

1. 11 yes   2. 88 no   103

Have you ever held back a sexual climax for fear of urinating?

1. 17 yes   2. 81 no   121

If you thought you had urinated, how did you feel about it?

1. 32 content   2. 27 ashamed   3. 39 other (specify)   44

If you thought your partner urinated, how did you feel about it?

1. 32 content   2. 3 ashamed   3. 9 disgusted

4. 56 other   34

°Number of respondents rather than percent on this item.

Number of
respondents
who answered
item

If female, do you experience a climax through intercourse without special clitoral stimulation?
   1. **40** yes   2. **25** no   3. **35** occasionally   104
          Note: 40 + 35 = 75 percent!

If male, does your present most important partner experience a climax through intercourse without special clitoral stimulation?
   1. **63** yes   2. **29** no   3. **4** occasionally   24

Do you distinguish between clitoral and vaginal climaxes?
   1. **55** yes   2. **35** no   3. **10** don't know   129

Do you (or your partner) experience:
   1. **12** clitoral climax   2. **8** vaginal climax
   3. **78** both   107

If you (or your partner) experience both, which do you prefer?
   1. **4** clitoral   2. **37** vaginal   3. **58** both   97

Do you (or does your partner) experience more than one kind of vaginal climax?
   1. **26** yes   2. **32** no   3. **42** don't know   107

Do you (or does your partner) experience climax as a result of a combination of clitoral and vaginal stimulation?
   1. **84** yes   2. **7** no   3. **9** don't know   121

If yes, which kind of climax do you (or does your partner) prefer?
   1. **6** clitoral   2. **22** vaginal   3. **34** mixed
   4. **35** all three   106
          Note: 34 + 35 = 69 percent!

As a result of clitoral stimulation, do you (or does your partner) experience:
   1. **33** climax   2. **20** an orgasm   3. **41** both at
different times   4. **1** neither   111

As a result of vaginal penetration, do you (or does your partner) experience:
   1. **8** a climax   2. **30** an orgasm   3. **36** both at
different times   4. **23** neither   116

Number of
respondents
who answered
item

When there is combined stimulation of the clitoris and vaginal penetration, do you (or does your partner) experience:

    1. **10** a climax   2. **34** an orgasm   3. **43** both
at different times   4. **9** neither   117

Do you (or does your partner) prefer:

    1. **7** clitoral stimulation   2. **17** vaginal
stimulation   3. **4** neither   4. **70** both   122

Do you (or does your partner) prefer:

    1. **6** a climax   2. **49** an orgasm   3. **41** both at
different times   108

Do/did you (or does/did your partner) ever use a diaphragm?

    1. **63** yes   2. **37** no   123

If yes, did the use of the diaphragm change your experience of climax
through intercourse?

    1. **20** yes   2. **25** no   3. **21** sometimes
4. **34** don't know   87

If yes, how? (Check any that apply.)*

    11   Did not reach orgasm as easily

    6   Did not reach orgasm at all

    20   Response was less intense

    0   Did not ejaculate

Did you (or did your partner) ever experience an "inner" or vaginal
climax without having an orgasm?

    1. **30** yes   2. **18** no   3. **50** don't know   109

If you (or your partner) has a specially sensitive spot in the vagina,
what factors play a role in whether it is reached and stimulated?
(Check any that apply.)

    32   Length of man's penis

    25   Circumference of man's penis

    33   Angle of erect penis

    11   Whether or not I am wearing a diaphragm

    36   Use of fingers

*Number of respondents rather than percent on this item.

Number of
respondents
who answered
item

77 Position used in intercourse
56 Depth of my involvement with partner
55 Ability of my partner to move his pelvis
61 My ability to move my pelvis

If length of penis is important, which reaches the spot most easily?
 0 short penis **32** medium penis **44** long
penis **20** don't know   50

If circumference of penis is important, which width best reaches the spot?
 2 narrow **30** medium **43** wide **25** don't know 44

If diaphragm is a factor, which stimulates the spot most easily?
 1. **0** with diaphragm 2. **96** without diaphragm 24

If use of fingers is a factor, which stimulates spot most easily?
 1. **51** fingers 2. **40** penis 3. **2** other (specify) 47

If position in intercourse is important, which position reaches spot more easily? (Check any that apply.)*

49 Woman on top of man
52 Man on top of woman (face to face)
16 Man on top of woman with woman lying on stomach
18 Man on top of woman with woman on knees

Please make any additional comments you would like about the questionnaire or its subject matter:

Conclusion

In spite of prevailing opinion that opposed or ignored many of the beliefs in this questionnaire, e.g. a sensitive spot in the vagina, female ejaculation, different types of orgasms, substantial numbers of professionals believed in the existence of these phenomena. Thus, the findings of this study provide additional confirmation of the laboratory results of Perry and Whipple, and in addition add to our knowledge of the continuum from climax to orgasm.

*Number of respondents rather than percent on this item.

Reference Notes

Introduction

1 Solomon E. Asch, "Studies of Independence and Conformity," pp. 1–70. Alice K. Ladas, "Breastfeeding: The Less Available Option," pp. 317–346.

1. A New Synthesis

1. Leah Schaefer, "A History of the Society for the Scientific Study of Sex."

2. Books of "minor morals" were published in Victorian England as guides to the manners, conventions, and etiquette of the times.

3. Richard von Krafft-Ebing, *Psychopathia Sexualis*.

4. Sigmund Freud, "The Voice of Sigmund Freud."

5. Sigmund Freud, "New Introductory Lectures on Psycho-Analysis," p. 135.

6. Karen Horney, "The Flight from Womanhood," p. 72.

7. Margaret Mead, *Male and Female*, pp. 217–218.

8. Edward Brecher, *The Sex Researchers*, p. 105.

9. Ibid., p. 117. See Wardell B. Pomeroy, et al., *Taking a Sexual History*.

10. Alfred C. Kinsey, Wardell B. Pomeroy, Clyde E. Martin, and Paul H. Gebhard, *Sexual Behavior in the Human Female*, pp. 574–580.

11. Zwi Hoch, "The Sensory Arm of the Female Orgasmic Reflex," p. 6.

12. Alice K. Ladas and Harold S. Ladas, "Women and Bioenergetic Analysis," pp. 5–8.

13. Martin Weisberg, "A Note on Female Ejaculation," p. 90.

14. J. Lowndes Sevely and J. W. Bennett, "Concerning Female Ejaculation and the Female Prostate," pp. 10–15.

15. Edwin G. Belzer, Jr., "Orgasmic Expulsions of Women," pp. 10–11.

2. The Gräfenberg Spot

1. Ernst Gräfenberg and Robert L. Dickinson, "Conception Control by Plastic Cervix Cap," pp. 337–338.

2. Ernst Gräfenberg, "The Role of Urethra in Female Orgasm" (1950), p. 146.

3. Gräfenberg's observations were also confirmed more recently by Hoch: "In a consistently recurrent manner, the anterior vaginal wall was found to be extremely sensitive and excitable with a lighter but still very similar intensity, although somewhat different quality than that of the clitoris . . . and in some of the women stimulation of the anterior vaginal wall proved to be even more effective than direct clitoral stimulation." Zwi Hoch, "The Sensory Arm of the Female Orgasmic Reflex," p. 5.

4. Ernst Gräfenberg, "The Role of Urethra" (1953), p. 119.

5. A. C. Kinsey, W. B. Pomeroy, C. E. Martin, and P. H. Gebhard, Sexual Behavior in the Human Female, p. 580.

6. Ernst Gräfenberg, "The Role of Urethra" (1953), p. 118.

7. Ibid., p. 119.

8. Elaine Morgan, The Descent of Woman, pp. 85–86.

9. Ernst Gräfenberg, "The Role of Urethra" (1953), p. 119.

10. Bronislaw Malinowski, The Sexual Life of Savages, p. 398.

11. William Masters, paper presented to the Fourteenth National Meeting of the American Association of Sex Educators, Counselors, and Therapists. San Francisco: April 4, 1981.

12. Federation of Feminists Women's Health Centers, A New View of a Woman's Body, p. 43.

13. Zwi Hoch, "The Sensory Arm," p. 6.

14. Ernst Gräfenberg, "The Role of Urethra in Female Orgasm" (1950), p. 146.

15. Ernst Gräfenberg and Robert L. Dickinson, "Conception Control," pp. 337–338.

16. Regnier de Graaf, *New Treatise Concerning the Generative Organs of Women*, pp. 103–107.

17. John D. Perry, Beverly Whipple, and Edwin G. Belzer, "Female Ejaculation by Digital Stimulation of the Gräfenberg Spot," p. 10.

18. Franklin P. Johnson, "The Homologue of the Prostate in the Female," p. 14.

19. George T. Caldwell, "The Glands of the Posterior Female Urethra," pp. 631–632.

20. John W. Huffman, "Clinical Significance of the Paraurethral Ducts and Glands," p. 615.

21. Alfred I. Folsom and Harold A. O'Brien, "The Female Obstructing Prostate," p. 375.

22. Huffman again published papers in 1948 and 1951 concerning the anatomy of the paraurethral ducts and their clinical significance. There are "numerous" (rather than two, as described by Skene) "ducts and epithelial-lined pockets which empty into the distal third of the female urethra." (John W. Huffman, "Clinical Significance," p. 615.) He viewed them as a homologue of the male prostate although he was solely concerned with clinical problems, not with pleasure.

In 1950, three physicians confirmed Huffman's view that Skene's glands were more extensive than Skene had imagined, and that they "penetrated deeply into the urethrovaginal wall" and sometimes "extended as far as the middle third of the urethra." (J. V. Ricci, J. R. Lisa, and C. H. Thom, "The Female Urethra," p. 505.) They called attention to the fact that the outer third of the urethra has a vascular plexus and the middle third a layer of muscle bundles well supplied with blood vessels.

23. Samuel Gordon Berkow, "The Corpus Spongeosum of the Urethra," p. 350.

24. John D. Perry and Beverly Whipple, "Female Ejaculation by Gräfenberg Spot Stimulation: A Special Presentation," p. 10.

3. Female Ejaculation

1. Regnier de Graaf, *New Treatise Concerning the Generative Organs of Women*, p. 107.

2. Edwin G. Belzer, "Orgasmic Expulsions of Women," p. 6.

3. Theodore H. van de Velde, *Ideal Marriage*, p. 178.

4. Phil Kilbraten, anthropologist, Bryn Mawr College, personal communication, April 26, 1980.

5. Ernst Gräfenberg, "The Role of Urethra in Female Orgasm," (1950), p. 147.

6. Ibid., p. 147.

7. Frank Addiego et al., "Female Ejaculation: A Case Study," p. 9. The results of the composition of ejaculate and urine specimens reported in this case study are displayed in the following table:

Comparison of the Composition of Ejaculate and Urine Specimens[1]

Specimens	Prostatic acid phosphatase (Sigma units/ml)	Urea (mMol/1)	Creatinine (µMol/1)	Glucose (mg/100 ml)
Ejaculate				
1	21.25	125.0	1780.0	21.5
2	8.55	27.0	1070.0	37.0
3	33.00	†	†	48.0
4	23.75	80.0	3800.0	54.0
M	21.6	77.3	2216.7	40.1
SD	10.1	49.1	1416.4	14.3
Urine				
5	0.15	240.0	14000.0	50.0
6	0.15	160.0	9600.0	3.5
7	0.10	204.0	14000.0	3.5
M	0.13	201.0	12533.0	19.0
SD	0.03	40.0	2540.0	26.8
t(df)‡	3.60(5)**	3.39 (4)*	6.14 (4)**	1.36 (5)

† not determined due to insufficient sample. $*p < .05.$
‡ one-tailed test. $**p < .01.$

[1] Prostatic acid phosphatase levels were determined using the Tartaric Acid Inhibition test.

8. J. Lowndes Sevely and J. W. Bennett, "Concerning Female Ejaculation and the Female Prostate," p. 1.

9. Ibid., p. 6. The homologues in the female and male anatomy can be seen in their table:

Homologues in Female and Male Urogenital Anatomy*

Adult female	*Adult male*
Ovary	Testis
Vagina (upper)	Vagina masculina
Uterus	Prostatic utricle
Fallopian tubes	Appendix testis
Canals and ducts of Gartner	Seminal vesicles
	Vas deferens
	Epididymis
Bladder	Bladder
Urethra	Prostatic urethra
Vestibule	Penile urethra
Labia minora	Urethral tube of penis
Labia majora	Scrotum
Clitoris	Penis
Bartholin's glands (vestibular glands)	Cowper's glands (bulbourethral glands)
Prostate gland (urethral glands)	Prostate gland (urethral glands)

*Adapted from Money (1952), Moore (1974), and Sevely (Note 1).

10. William Masters and Virginia Johnson, *Human Sexual Response*, p. 135.

11. Alfred Kinsey et al., *Sexual Behavior in the Human Female*, pp. 634–635.

12. Germaine Greer, *The Female Eunuch*, p. 240.

13. J. Lowndes Sevely and J. W. Bennett, Ibid., p. 17.

14. Bronislaw Malinowski, *The Sexual Life of Savages*, pp. 167–168.

15. John D. Perry and Beverly Whipple, "Can Women Ejaculate? Yes!" p. 55.

4. *The Importance of Healthy Pelvic Muscles*

1. Helen Singer Kaplan, *The New Sex Therapy*, pp. 26–31.

2. Elizabeth Noble, *Essential Exercises for the Childbearing Years*.

3. W. J. Brown, "Microbial Flora in Infections of the Vagina," p. 423. The observation of a possible relationship between pelvic muscle tension and urinary tract infections has recently been confirmed by a urologist: see R. A. Schmidt and E. A. Tanagho, "Urethral Syndrome or Urinary Tract Infection?," pp. 424–427.

4. Thomas H. Green, "Urinary Stress Incontinence," pp. 368–400. Also E. A. Graber, "Stress Incontinence in Women," pp. 565–577.

5. Martin Weisberg, "Lax Vaginal Muscles," pp. 9–10.

6. Theodore H. van de Velde, *Ideal Marriage*, p. 60.

7. Ibid., p. 70.

8. Arnold H. Kegel, "Stress Incontinence of Urine in Women," pp. 487–499.

9. Georgia Kline-Graber and Benjamin Graber, *Women's Orgasm*, p. 77.

10. Georgia Kline-Graber and Benjamin Graber, "Female Orgasm: Role of the Pubococcygeus Muscle," pp. 348–351. See also: Benjamin Graber (ed.), *Circumvaginal Musculature and Sexual Function*.

11. John D. Perry and Beverly Whipple, "Pelvic Muscle Strength of Female Ejaculators: Evidence in Support of a New Theory of Orgasm," pp. 22–39. The twenty four ejaculators averaged 12 microvolts with vaginal myography, compared with 7 microvolts for the twenty-three nonejaculators; a statistically significant difference (p = .0005). Kegel's figures were in millimeters of mercury and tend to be about twice as high as our microvolt figures. Also see "Vaginal Myography," chapter 5, in Benjamin Graber (ed.), *Circumvaginal Musculature*.

12. Cyril Fox, "Some Aspects and Implications of Coital Physiology," pp. 205–213; Cyril Fox and Beatrice Fox, "A Comparative Study of Coital Physiology," pp. 319–336; and Cyril Fox, H. S. Wolff, and J. A. Baker, "Measurement of Intra-Vaginal and Intra-Uterine Pressures During Human Coitus by Radio-Telemetry," pp. 243–251.

13. Theodore H. van de Velde, *Ideal Marriage*, p. 70.

14. Bronislaw Malinowski, *The Sexual Life of Savages*, p. 398.
15. Alexander Lowen, *Movement and Feeling in Sex*, p. 739.

5. New Understandings of Human Orgasm

1. Roger Williams, *Biochemical Individuality*, p. ix.
2. Alfred C. Kinsey, Wardell B. Pomeroy, and Clyde E. Martin, *Sexual Behavior in the Human Male*, p. 639.
3. Irving Singer, *The Goals of Human Sexuality*, p. 15.
4. James L. McCary, *Human Sexuality*, p. 86.
5. Irving Singer, *The Goals of Human Sexuality*, Chapter 5.
6. Alfred C. Kinsey et al., *Sexual Behavior*, p. 386.
7. Josephine and Irving Singer, "Types of Female Orgasm," p. 4.
8. In France, Gilbert Tordjman concluded that "deeper" orgasms, such as Freud described, were possible based on his reading of effects of spinal cord injuries; see "New Realities in the Study of the Female's Orgasm," *Journal of Sex Education and Therapy*, pp. 22–26. In California, biologist Julian Davidson developed a "bipolar" hypothesis of orgasm based on the Singer theory and research into altered states of consciousness; see "Psychobiology of Sexual Experience," *Psychobiology of Consciousness*, pp. 309–310.
9. John D. Perry and Beverly Whipple, "Two Devices for the Physiological Measurement of Sexual 'Activity.'"
10. John D. Perry and Beverly Whipple, "Multiple Components of the Female Orgasm," Chapter 9.
11. Patricia Gillan and G. S. Brindley, "Vaginal and Pelvic Floor Responses to Sexual Stimulation," pp. 471–481.
12. Mary Jo Sholty, "Female Subjective Sexual Experience."
13. Julian Davidson, "The Psychobiology of Sexual Experience," p. 303.
14. Alexander Lowen, *Love and Orgasm*, p. 217.
15. Mina B. Robbins and Gordon D. Jensen, "Multiple Orgasms in Male," pp. 21–26.
16. Wilhelm Reich, *The Function of the Orgasm*, pp. 72–87.
17. Alexander Lowen and Leslie Lowen, *The Way to Vibrant Health*, p. 7.
18. Alexander Lowen, "Movement and Feeling in Sex," p. 741.

6. *The Best Is the Enemy of the Good*

1. Michael Carrera, *Sex*, p. 95.
2. Helen S. Kaplan, *The New Sex Therapy*.
3. Seymour Fisher, *Understanding the Female Orgasm*, p. 221.
4. Cynthia Jayne, "A Two-Dimensional Model of Female Sexual response."
5. Shere Hite, *The Hite Report*, pp. 57–63.
6. Mina B. Robbins and Gordon D. Jensen, "Multiple Orgasm in Males," p. 23.
7. Avodah K. Offit, *The Sexual Self*, p. 12.
8. Luciano Pavarotti and William Wright, *Pavarotti: My Own Story*, p. 33.
9. W. Timothy Gallwey, *The Inner Game of Tennis*, p. 13.
10. Avodah K. Offit, p. 29.

Bibliography

Addiego, Frank; Belzer, Edwin G., Jr.; Comolli, Jill; Moger, William; Perry, John D.; and Whipple, Beverly. "Female Ejaculation: A Case Study," *The Journal of Sex Research*, 17 (1981): 13–21.

Asch, Solomon E. "Studies of Independence and Conformity, A Minority of One Against a Unanimous Majority," *Psychological Monographs*, 70 (1956): 1–70.

Austen, Leo. "Procreation Among the Trobriand Islanders," *Oceania*, 5 (1934–1935): 102–113.

Barbach, Lonnie Garfield. *For Yourself—The Fulfillment of Female Sexuality*. New York: Doubleday, 1975.

Beach, Frank A. (ed.) *Human Sexuality in Four Perspectives*. Baltimore: Johns Hopkins University Press, 1977.

Belzer, Edwin G., Jr. "Orgasmic Expulsions of Women: A Review and Heuristic Inquiry," *The Journal of Sex Research*, 17: (1981) 1–12

Bergler, Edmund. "The Problem of Frigidity," *Psychiatric Quarterly*, 18 (1944): 374–390.

Berkow, Samuel G. "The Corpus Spongeosum of the Urethra: Its Possible Role in Urinary Control and Stress Incontinence in Women," *American Journal of Obstetrics and Gynecology*, 65 (1953): 346–351.

Bohlen, Joseph G., and Held, J. P. "An Anal Probe for Monitoring Vascular and Muscular Events During Sexual Response," *Psychophysiology*, 16 (1979): 318–323.

Bonaparte, Marie. *Female Sexuality*. New York: International Universities Press, 1953.

Brecher, Edward. *The Sex Researchers*. San Francisco, Specific Press, 1979.

Brecher, Ruth, and Brecher, Edward. *An Analysis of Human Sexual Response*. New York: Signet Books, 1966.

Brown, W. J. "Microbial Flora in Infections of the Vagina." In *The Human Vagina*, edited by E. S. E. Hafex and T. N. Evans. Amsterdam: Elsevier/North Holland Biomedical Press, 1978.

Bychowski, G. "Some Aspects of Psychosexuality in Psychoanalytic Experience." In *Psychosexual Development in Health and Disease*, edited by P. H. Hoc and J. Zubin. New York: Grune and Stratton, 1949.

Calderone, Mary S., and Johnson, Eric W. *The Family Book About Sexuality*. New York: Harper & Row, 1981.

Caldwell, George T. "The Glands of the Posterior Female Urethra," *Texas State Journal of Medicine*, 36 (1941): 627–632.

Campbell, B., and Petersen, W. E. "Milk 'Let-down' and the Orgasm in the Human Female." *Human Biology*, 25 (1953): 165–168.

Carrera, Michael. *Sex: The Facts, the Acts and Your Feelings*. New York: Crown, 1981.

Clark, R. *Freud: The Man and the Cause*. New York: Random House, 1981.

Curtis, A. H.; Anson, B. J.; and Chester, B. M. "The Anatomy of the Pelvic and Urogenital Diaphragms, in Relation to Urethrocele and Cystocele," *Surgery, Gynecology and Obstetrics*, 68 (1939): 161–166.

Davidson, Julian. "The Psychobiology of Sexual Experience." In *Psychobiology of Consciousness*, edited by J. and R. Davidson. New York: Plenum Press, 1980, pp. 309–310.

De Graaf, Regnier. (1672) "New Treatise Concerning the Generative Organs of Women." In *Journal of Reproduction and Fertility*, Supplement No. 17, 77–222. H. B. Jocelyn and B. P. Setchell, eds. Oxford, England: Blackwell Scientific Publications, 1972.

Deutsch, H. *The Psychology of Woman* (Vol. 1 and 2). New York: Grune and Stratton, 1945.

Dickinson, Robert L. *Atlas of Human Sexual Anatomy.* (Facsimile edition of 1949 original.) New York: Robert E. Krieger, 1971.

Ellis, Albert. "Is the Vaginal Orgasm a Myth?" In *Sex, Society and the Individual*, edited by A. P. Pillay and A. E. Ellis. Bombay: International Journal of Sexology, 1953.

Federation of Feminists Women's Health Centers. *A New View of a Woman's Body.* New York: Simon and Schuster, 1981.

Fischer, Ann. "Reproduction in Truk," *Ethnology: An International Journal of Cultural and Social Anthropology*, 2 (1963): 526–540.

Fisher, Seymour. *Understanding the Female Orgasm.* New York: Bantam Books, 1973.

Fisher, Seymour. *The Female Orgasm: Psychology, Physiology, Fantasy.* New York: Basic Books, 1973.

Folsom, Alfred I., and O'Brien, Harold A. "The Female Obstructing Prostate," *Journal of the American Medical Association*, 121 (1943): 573–580.

Ford, Clellan S., and Beach, Frank A. *Patterns of Sexual Behavior.* New York: Harper and Brothers, 1952.

Fox, Cyril. "Some Aspects and Implications of Coital Physiology," *Journal of Sex and Marital Therapy*, 2 (1976): 205–213.

Fox, Cyril, and Fox, Beatrice. "A Comparative Study of Coital Physiology with Special Reference to the Sexual Climax," *Journal of Reproductive Fertility*, 24 (1971): 319–336.

Fox, Cyril; Wolff, H. S.; and Baker, J. A. "Measurement of Intra-Vaginal and Intra-Uterine Pressures During Human Coitus by Radio-Telemetry," *Journal of Reproduction and Fertility*, 22 (1970): 243–251.

Francoeur, Robert T. *Becoming a Sexual Person.* New York: John Wiley and Sons, 1982.

Freud, Sigmund. (1905) *Three Essays on the Theory of Sexuality.* Standard Edition. London: Hogarth Press 7 (1953): 125–245.

Freud, Sigmund. (1905) *Three Contributions to the Theory of Sex.* In *Basic Writings of Sigmund Freud*, edited by A. A. Brill, New York: Modern Library, Inc. 1938.

Freud, Sigmund. (1917) *General Theory of the Neurosis*. Standard Edition 16 (1963):

Freud, Sigmund. (1920) *Beyond the Pleasure Principle*. Standard Edition. London: Hogarth Press 18 (1955): 3–64.

Freud, Sigmund. (1923) *Some Psychical Consequences of the Anatomical Distinction Between the Sexes*. Standard Edition 19 (1961): 248–258.

Freud, Sigmund (1926) *The Question of Lay Analysis, Conversations with an Impartial Person*. Standard Edition. London: Hogarth Press 20 (1953): 183–258.

Freud, Sigmund. (1933) *New Introductory Lectures on Psycho-Analysis: Femininity*. Standard Edition. London: Hogarth Press 22 (1964): 112–135.

Freud, Sigmund. "The Voice of Sigmund Freud." Recorded in 1938, introduced by Marie Coleman Nelson and produced by the National Psychological Association for Psychoanalysis.

Gallwey, W. Timothy *The Inner Game of Tennis*. New York: Random House, 1974.

Gillan, P. "Objective Measures of Female Sexual Arousal," *Proceedings of the Physiological Society*, 260 (1976): 64–65.

Gillan, P., and Brindley, G. S. "Vaginal and Pelvic Floor Responses to Sexual Stimulation," *Psychophysiology*, 16:5 (1979): 471–481.

Gladwin, Thomas, and Sarason, Seymour B. *Truk: Man in Paradise*. Viking Fund Publications in Anthropology, 20. New York: Werner-Gren Foundation for Anthropological Research, 1954.

Goff, Byron H. "An Histological Study of the Perivaginal Fascia in a Nullipara," *Surgery, Gynecology and Obstetrics*, 52:1 (1931): 32–42.

Goodenough, Ward H. *Premarital Freedom on Truk: Theory and Practice*. American Anthropological Association, 1949.

Graber, A. "Stress Incontinence in Women: A Review," *Obstetrics/ Gynecology Survey*, 32 (1977): 565–577.

Graber, Benjamin. *Circumvaginal Musculature and Sexual Function*. New York: S. Karger, 1982.

Graber, Benjamin, and Kline-Graber, Georgia. "Female Orgasm: Role of the Pubococcygeus," *Journal of Clinical Psychiatry*, 40 (1979): 34–39.

Gräfenberg, Ernst. "The Role of Urethra in Female Orgasm," *International Journal of Sexology*, 3 (1950): 145–148.

Gräfenberg, Ernst. "The Role of Urethra in Female Orgasm," in *Sex, Society and the Individual*, edited by A. Pillay and A. Ellis. Bombay: *International Journal of Sexology*, 3 (1953): 118–120.

Gräfenberg, Ernst, and Dickinson, Robert L. "Conception Control by Plastic Cervix Cap," *Western Journal of Surgery, Obstetrics and Gynecology*, 52 (1944): 335–340.

Green, Thomas H. "Urinary Stress Incontinence: Differential Diagnosis, Pathophysiology, and Management," *American Journal of Obstetrics and Gynecology*, 122 (1975): 368–400.

Greer, Germaine. *The Female Eunuch*. New York: Bantam Books, 1970.

Hartman, William E., and Fithian, Marilyn A. *Treatment of Sexual Dysfunction*. New York: Jason Aronson, 1974.

Henson, C.; Rubin, H. B.; and Henson, D. E. "Women's Sexual Arousal Concurrently Assessed by Three Genital Measures," *Archives of Sexual Behavior*, 8 (1979): 459–469.

Hite, Shere. *The Hite Report*. New York: Collier Macmillan Publishers, 1976.

Hoch, Zwi. "The Sensory Arm of the Female Orgasmic Reflex," *Journal of Sex Education and Therapy*, 6 (1980): 4–7.

Hoon, E. F.; Hoon, P. W.; and Wincze, J. P. "An Inventory for the Measurement of Female Sexual Arousability: The SAI," *Archives of Sexual Behavior*, 5 (1976): 291–300.

Horney, Karen. "The Denial of the Vagina," *International Journal of Psychoanalysis* 14 (1933): 47–70.

Horney, Karen. *Feminine Psychology*. New York: Norton Library, 1967.

Horney, Karen. "The Flight from Womanhood: The Masculinity-Complex in Women as Viewed by Men and by Women," In *Sex Differences*, edited by P. Lee and R. S. Stuart, New York: Urizen Books, 1976, pp. 57–73.

Huffman , John W. "The Detailed Anatomy of the Paraurethral Ducts in the Adult Human Female," *American Journal of Obstetrics and Gynecology*, 55 (1948): 86–101.

Huffman, John W. "The Development of the Paraurethral Glands in the Human Female," *American Journal of Obstetrics and Gynecology*, 46 (1943): 773–785.

Huffman, John W. "Clinical Significance of the Paraurethral Ducts and Glands," *Archives of Surgery*, 62 (1951): 615–626.

Janeway, Elizabeth. "Who Is Sylvia? On the Loss of Sexual Paradigms." In *Women: Sex and Sexuality*, edited by Catharine Stimpson and Ethel Spector Person. Chicago: University of Chicago Press, 1980.

Jayne, Cynthia. "A Two-Dimensional Model of Female Sexual Response," *Journal of Sex and Marital Therapy*, 7 (1981): 3–30.

Johnson, Franklin P. "The Homologue of the Prostate in the Female," *Journal of Urology*, 8 (1922): 13–33.

Johnson, Warren R., and Belzer, Edwin G., Jr. *Human Sexual Behavior and Sex Education: With Historical, Moral, Legal, Linguistic, and Cultural Perspectives*. Philadelphia: Lea and Febiger, 1973.

Kaplan, Helen S. *The New Sex Therapy*. New York: Brunner/Mazel, 1974.

Kaplan, Helen S. *Illustrated Manual of Sex Therapy*. New York: Quadrangle Books, 1975.

Kegel, Arnold H. "Progressive Resistance Exercise in the Functional Restoration of the Perineal Muscles," *American Journal of Obstetrics and Gynecology*, 56 (1948): 238–248.

Kegel, Arnold H. "The Physiologic Treatment of Poor Tone and Function of the Genital Muscles and of Urinary Stress Incontinence," *Western Journal of Surgery, Obstetrics, and Gynecology*, 57 (1949): 527–535.

Kegel, Arnold H. "Stress Incontinence and Genital Relaxation," *CIBA Clinical Symposium*, 4 (1952): 35–51.

Kegel, Arnold H. "Sexual Functions of the Pubococcygeus Muscle," *Western Journal of Surgery, Obstetrics, and Gynecology*, 60 (1952): 521–524.

Kegel, Arnold H. "Stress Incontinence of Urine in Women: Physiologic Treatment," *Journal of the International College of Surgeons*, 25 (1956): 487–499.

Kegel, Arnold H. "Early Genital Relaxation," *Obstetrics and Gynecology*, 8 (1956): 245–250.

Kegel, Arnold H. *Pathologic Physiology of the Pubococcygeus Mus-*

cle in Women 1956. Film available from Morgan Camera Shop, 6262 Sunset Boulevard, Hollywood, CA 90028.

Kelly, G. L. *Sex Manual.* Eighth edition. Augusta, Georgia: Southern Medical Supply Co., 1959.

Kinsey, Alfred C.; Pomeroy, Wardell B.; and Martin, Clyde E. *Sexual Behavior in the Human Male.* Philadelphia: W. B. Saunders, 1948.

Kinsey, Alfred C.; Pomeroy, Wardell B.; Martin, Clyde E.; and Gebhard, Paul H. *Sexual Behavior in the Human Female.* Philadelphia: W. B. Saunders Co., 1953.

Kline-Graber, Georgia, and Graber, Benjamin. "Diagnosis and Treatment Procedures of Pubococcygeus Deficiencies in Women." In *Handbook of Sex Therapy* J. LoPiccolo and L. LoPiccolo (eds.), New York: Plenum Press, 1978.

Kline-Graber, Georgia, and Graber, Benjamin. *Woman's Orgasm: A Guide to Sexual Satisfaction.* New York: Popular Library, 1975.

Krafft-Ebing, Richard von. *Psychopathia Sexualis.* Translated by F. J. Rebman. Brooklyn, N.Y.: Physicians and Suregeons Book Co., 1922.

Krantz, K. E. "Anatomy of the Urethra and Anterior Vaginal Wall," *Transactions of the American Association of Obstetricians, Gynecologists, and Abdominal Surgeons,* 61 (1950): 31–59.

Kronhausen, P., and Kronhausen, E. *The Sexually Responsive Woman.* New York: Grove Press, 1964.

Ladas, Alice K. "Breastfeeding: The Less Available Option." *The Journal of Tropical Pediatrics and Environmental Child Health,* 18 (1972): 317–346.

Ladas, Alice K., and Ladas, Harold S. "Women and Bioenergetic Analysis." Monograph published by the Connecticut Society for Bioenergetic Analysis, Newington, Conn., 1981. 27 pp.

Ladas, Alice K. "What Professionals Believe About Female Sexual Response." Unpublished manuscript.

Lehfeldt, Hans. "Ernst Gräfenberg, and His Ring," *The Mt. Sinai Journal of Medicine,* 42 (1975): 345–352.

Levitt, E. E.; Knoovsky, M.; Freese, M. P.; and Thompson, J. F. "Intravaginal Pressure Assessed by the Kegel Perineometer," *Archives of Sexual Behavior,* 8 (1979): 425–430.

Logan, T. G. "The Vaginal Clasp: A Method of Comparing Contractions Across Subjects," *The Journal of Sex Research*, 11 (1975): 353–358.

Lowen, Alexander. "Movement and Feeling in Sex." In *The Encyclopedia of Sexual Behavior*, edited by Albert Ellis and Albert Abarbanel. New York: Hawthorne Books, 1961.

Lowen, Alexander. *Love and Orgasm*. New York: Macmillan, 1965.

Lowen, Alexander. *Betrayal of the Body*. New York: Macmillan, 1967.

Lowen, Alexander. *Stress and Illness*. New York: International Institute for Bioenergetic Analysis, 1980.

Lowen, Alexander, and Lowen, Leslie. *The Way to Vibrant Health: A Manual of Bioenergetic Exercises*. New York: Harper & Row, 1977.

Malinowski, Bronislaw. *The Sexual Life of Savages*. New York: Harcourt Brace & World, 1929.

Maly, Betty Joan. "Rehabilitation Principles in the Care of Gynecologic and Obstetric Patients," *Archives of Physical Medicine and Rehabilitation*, 61 (1980): 78–81.

Mandelstam, D. "The Pelvic Floor," *Physiotherapy*, August, 1978.

Marmor, J. "Some Considerations Concerning Orgasm in the Female," *Psychosomatic Medicine*, 16 (1954): 240–245.

Masters, William H., and Johnson, Virginia. "Anatomy of the Female Orgasm." In *The Encyclopedia of Sexual Behavior*, edited by A. Ellis and A. Abarbanel. New York: Hawthorne, 1961.

Masters, William H., and Johnson, Virginia E. *Human Sexual Response*. Boston: Little, Brown, 1966.

Masters, William. Paper presented at the Fourteenth National Meeting of the American Association of Sex Educators, Counselors, and Therapists. San Francisco, April 4, 1981.

McCary, James L. *Human Sexuality*. 2nd ed. New York: Van Nostrand, 1973.

McCary, James L. *McCary's Human Sexuality*. New York: Van Nostrand, 1978.

Mead, Margaret. *Male and Female: A Study of the Sexes in a Changing World*. New York: William Morrow, 1939.

Mead, Margaret. *From the South-Seas: Studies of Adolescence and Sex in Primitive Societies*. New York: William Morrow, 1939.

Money, J., and Tucker, P. *Sexual Signatures: On Being a Man or a Woman*. Boston: Little, Brown, 1975.

Morgan, Elaine. *Descent of Woman*. New York: Stein & Day, 1972.

Mould, Douglas E. "Neuromuscular Aspects of Women's Orgasms," *The Journal of Sex Research*, 16 (1980): 197–201.

Noble, Elizabeth. *Essential Exercises for the Childbearing Years*. Rev. ed. Boston: Houghton Mifflin, 1982.

Offit, Avodah K. *The Sexual Self*. Philadelphia: J. B. Lippincott, 1977.

Pavarotti, Luciano, and Wright, William. *Pavarotti: My Own Story*. New York: Doubleday, 1981.

Perry, John D., and Whipple, Beverly. "Can Women Ejaculate? Yes!," *Forum, The International Journal of Human Relations*. April, 1981, 54–58.

Perry, John D., and Whipple, Beverly. "Female Ejaculation by Gräfenberg Spot Stimulation," a "special presentation" at the annual meeting of The Society for the Scientific Study of Sex, Dallas, November 15, 1980.

Perry, John D., and Whipple, Beverly. "If Your Sexual Response is Poor, the Cause Could Be Weak PC Muscles," *Forum, The International Journal of Human Relations*. January, 1981, 51–55.

Perry, John D., and Whipple, Beverly. "Multiple Components of the Female Orgasm." In *Circumvaginal Musculature and Sexual Function*, edited by Benjamin Graber. New York: S. Karger, 1982.

Perry, John D., and Whipple, Beverly. "Pelvic Muscle Strength of Female Ejaculators: Evidence in Support of a New Theory of Orgasm," *The Journal of Sex Research*, 17 (1981): 22–39.

Perry, John D., and Whipple, Beverly. "Research Notes: The Varieties of Female Orgasm and Female Ejaculation," *SIECUS Report*, May–July, 1981, 15–16.

Perry, John D., and Whipple, Beverly. "Two Devices for the Physiological Measurement of Sexual Activity." Paper presented to the Eastern Regional Conference of the Society for the Scientific Study of Sex. April, 1980.

Perry, John D., and Whipple, Beverly. "Vaginal Myography." In *Circumvaginal Musculature and Sexual Function*, edited by Benjamin Graber. New York: S. Karger, 1982.

Perry, John D.; Whipple, Beverly; and Belzer, Edwin G. "Female Ejaculation by Digital Stimulation of the Gräfenberg Spot." Paper presented to the Society for the Scientific Study of Sex, Philadelphia, April 12, 1981.

Pomeroy, Wardell B.; Flax, Carol C.; and Wheeler, Connie Christine. *Taking a Sexual History: Interviewing and Recording.* Riverside, New Jersey: The Free Press, 1982.

Rado, S. "Sexual Anaesthesia in the Female," *Quarterly Review of Surgery, Obstetrics and Gynecology,* 16 (1959): 249–253.

Reich, Wilhelm. *The Function of the Orgasm.* Translated by Theodore Wolfe. New York: Orgone Institute Press, 1942.

Reich, Wilhelm. *Character Analysis.* Translated by Theodore Wolfe. New York: Orgone Institute Press, 1949.

Ricci, J. V.; Lisa, J. R.; and Thom, C. H. "The Female Urethra," *American Journal of Surgery,* 79 (1950): 449–506.

Robbins, Mina B., and Jensen, Gordon D. "Multiple Orgasm in Males," *The Journal of Sex Research,* 14 (1978): 21–26.

Robinson, M. *The Power of Sexual Surrender.* New York: Garden City, 1959.

Schaefer, Leah. "A History of The Society for the Scientific Study of Sex as a Reflection of Research Advances in Sexology." Paper presented to the Society for the Scientific Study of Sex, Philadelphia, April, 1981.

Schmidt, R. A., and Tanagho, E. A. "Urethral Syndrome or Urinary Tract Infection?" *Urology,* 18 (1981): 424–427.

Sevely, J. Lowndes, and Bennett, J. W. "Concerning Female Ejaculation and the Female Prostate," *Journal of Sex Research,* 14 (1978): 1–20.

Skene, A. J. C. "The Anatomy and Pathology of Two Important Glands of the Female Urethra," *American Journal of Obstetrics and Diseases of Women and Children,* 13 (1880): 265–270.

Sherfy, M. J. *The Nature and Evolution of Female Sexuality.* New York: Vintage Books, 1973.

Sholty, Mary Jo. "Female Subjective Sexual Experience: A Descriptive Study." M.S.W. thesis, University of Maryland, 1980.

Singer, Irving. *The Goals of Human Sexuality.* New York: Schocken Books, 1973.

Singer, Josephine, and Singer, Irving. "Types of Female Orgasm," *Journal of Sex Research*, 8 (1972): 255–67.

Thompson, C. *Psychoanalysis: Evolution and Development*. New York: Hermitage, 1950.

Tordjman, G. "New Realities in the Study of Female Orgasms," *Journal of Sex Education and Therapy*, 6 (1980): 22–26. Originally published in French under the title "Nouvelles acquisitions dans l'étude des orgasmes féminins," *Contraception, Fertility and Sexuality*, 7 (1979): 215–222.

Van de Velde, T. H. *Ideal Marriage: Its Physiology and Technique*. New York: Covici, Friede, 1930. Also, New York: Random House, 1965.

Weisberg, Martin. "A Note on Female Ejaculation," *The Journal of Sex Research*, 17 (1981): 90.

Weisberg, Martin. "Lax Vaginal Muscles," *Medical Aspects of Human Sexuality*, 10 (1976):9–10.

Whanton, Lawrence. "The Non-operative Treatment of Stress Incontinence in Women," *Journal of Urology*, 69 (1953): 511–518.

Whipple, Beverly (consultant), Schoen, Mark (filmmaker). "Orgasmic Expulsions of Fluid in the Sexually Stimulated Female." Film available from Focus International Inc., 1776 Broadway, New York, N.Y. 10019.

Williams, Roger J. *Biochemical Individuality: The Basis for the Genetotrophic Concept*. Austin: University of Texas Press, 1956.

Wilson, Strong, Clark, and Johns. *Human Sexuality: A Text with Readings*. New York: West Publishing, 1977.

Zilbergeld, Bernie. *Male Sexuality*. New York: Bantam, 1978.

Zingheim, P. K., and Sandman, C. A. "Discriminative Control of the Vaginal Vasomotor Response," *Biofeedback and Self-Regulation*, 3 (1978): 29–41.

Index

About the Authors

Alice Kahn Ladas, M.S.S., Ed.D., a licensed psychologist practicing in Manhattan and Armonk, New York, became interested, early in her career, in working directly with the body as well as with words. As an expression of a lifelong interest in preventive mental health, she taught the first course in this country in the Lamaze method of educated childbirth and worked with the La Leche League to find out how to help mothers breast-feed. A member of the Institute for Bioenergetic Analysis, which she helped found, and a charter member of the Society for the Scientific Study of Sex, on the boards of both groups as well as the board of the New York Association for Marriage and Family Therapy, she lived for most of her professional life with the dilemma this book helps to resolve. She has written widely on breast-feeding and conducted bioenergetic workshops throughout Western Europe and in the United States.

Beverly Whipple, R.N., M.Ed., is an AASECT-certified sex educator and sex counselor, as well as a sexologist certified by the American College of Sexologists. She is Assistant Professor of Nursing and Human Sexuality at Gloucester County College in Sewell, New Jersey, and an Instructor in Psychiatry and Human Behavior at Jefferson Medical College in Philadelphia. She has done extensive lecturing at professional conferences and colleges and medical schools throughout the country, and has also co-authored numerous articles about the research discussed in this book as well as articles about sexuality education for health professionals. She appeared as a featured guest on the Phil Donohue Show in 1981, and was named one of the People to Watch in 1982 by *Philadelphia* magazine.

John Delbert Perry, M.Div., Ph.D, is a psychologist (licensed in Vermont), a sexologist (certified by the American College of Sexologists), and a biofeedback practitioner (certified by the Biofeedback Certification Institute of America), as well as an ordained minister in the United Church of Christ. His professional life began with the writing of *The Coffee House Ministry* (1966). He has been a college chaplain, an assistant professor of psychology, and is now in private practice, specializing in vaginal myography and other innovative applications of biofeedback. He founded Health Technology, Inc., to promote research and development in this field.